Life, Lies, and Sex:

A User's Guide to
Being in a Body

Mikaya Heart

Library of Congress Control Number: 2014915503
CreateSpace Independent Publishing
North Charleston, South Carolina 29406

Deep-felt gratitude goes to
Suzanne Coutanceau for the cover picture,
Shay Stone for helping with the cover, and most of all
Dayana Jon Patterson who did a great deal of editing
and formatting, besides teaching me just about
everything I know.

Cover photo: Flame Robin
by Suzanne Coutanceau

Praise for

Life, Lies, and Sex:
A User's Guide to Being in a Body

"Mikaya Heart has done it again. She has engaged a quantity of tricky, esoteric subjects (life, lies, and sex) and speaking from the Heart words of truth with brilliant, yet simple clarity, enables readers to embrace truths of their own."

Dayana Jon Patterson, Spiritual Mentor,
Matrix Energetics Practitioner, Laughter Yoga Teacher

"Once again Mikaya Heart does not disappoint. If you want original ideas for new times, this is the book for you."

Bonnie Coleen, Host/Producer of the
Radio program, *Seeing Beyond*

"This book answers many basic questions about life in an open, loving way, so that people can lose their misconceptions about life, and thereby, gain the world."

Diane Tegarden, author of *How to Escape a*
Bad Marriage – A Self Help Divorce Book for Women

"*Life, Lies, and Sex* is a beautiful meditation on the spirituality of sexuality...and a must-read. Bravo!"

Richard Wagner, Ph.D., ACS

"If you are ready to wake up! This book is for you. Mikaya Heart's teachings focus on the flow of energy and the art of choice to help you uncover a higher purpose, offering essential information for leading a life with no limits. *Life, Lies, and Sex* is an outstanding book written from the heart."

Lisa Love, Artist, Author, Designer, and Community
Steward for the women's blog *My Shoes, My Story*

Contents

Chapter One
Truth and Delusion

Our world is going through a huge shift in planetary awareness that is presently manifesting for many of us as a pervading dissatisfaction with the way things have been. We are moving into a new paradigm in which we will think differently and experience life differently. We are looking for what we might refer to as a "higher purpose," trying to work out where we fit and why we are here. We want more out of life, which some call a spiritual connection. Unfortunately and understandably, a lot of people are put off by the word *spiritual*. Although I rarely use that word, many people will consider it relevant to this book, so let me start by defining it.

I am not talking about religions, which are institutions, and as such, can offer only limited help to seekers, since any sense of a higher purpose is always personal. Spirituality could be defined as a study of the nature of reality, starting from the belief that there is a force at work much greater than the individual self. Some call this *God*, a word that is regrettably loaded with irrelevant and misleading meaning. I call it life force. When we are in alignment with that greater force—the energy of life itself—our lives run more smoothly and easily, and we operate from a place of trust, knowing that we will always be in the right place at the right time, however that may manifest. We have a much broader perspective on life and death. Developing this awareness of the flow of life, which is always occurring in and around us, expands the limits of our perception, helping us to understand how to exercise the art of choice, or manifestation.

I differ from most spiritual belief systems in my approach to the physical aspects of being alive in a human body. We (whoever we are, and I go into that later) have specifically and consciously chosen to manifest this body and the personality to go with it. The idea of being human is to be absolutely present in this body, always honoring it, and always paying attention to the depths of wisdom it offers us. The body is our bridge between energetic, or spirit, forms and the physical world, and as such, it is a source of information that we need to listen to. We are learning to embody different states of consciousness—in other words, bring them into the reality of our daily lives. Sex, which starts with the body and—if we are able to commit to the fullness of the experience—takes us far beyond it, is one of the easiest pathways to a state of expanded consciousness. Failing to address this amazing potential is one of the great downfalls of many spiritual practices. This does not mean that I believe spiritual leaders should be having sex with their followers (that kind of behavior lacks integrity), but that we each individually can use sex as a personal playground for expanding our consciousness.

I frequently hear people say they are looking for a depth that is missing in our modern world. The words, "greater," "higher," or "deeper" are commonly used, although those comparatives are deceptive. We are searching for an awareness of something more than what is required in the average person's daily life. We can learn to develop this awareness. In truth, what we perceive with the five senses known as sight, hearing, smell, taste, and touch, is only a tiny percentage of what exists all around us in energetic form. I use the phrase *the vastness of being* to refer to this immense unseen reality. Getting in touch with it often brings a sensation of relief because the belief that this physical world is all there is can make a person feel trapped. On the other hand, trying to grasp the vastness with the mental faculties will probably produce an immediate sense of overwhelm.

There is a tendency to believe that in the past people were more in touch with this vastness of being and therefore ancient teachings can help us to access it. In any particular instance, that may be true and it may not. The teachings that many spiritual leaders are offering just aren't relevant to this culture any more. They were learned and developed hundreds and thousands of years ago for very different cultures and civilizations, and nowadays they often serve only to confuse us even more about the true nature of reality. In the West, human life has changed radically in the last fifty to two hundred years. Most of us have moved out of survival mode, and we easily grasp concepts that were impossible for people who were struggling to fulfill their basic needs from day to day. The present planetary shift is about an evolution of consciousness, a deep change in the way that we perceive reality. Any teacher must be able to reach us on that level, offering new and empowering ideas that help us to think for ourselves. We can no longer be fobbed off with the old trite answers. We're ready to move on to a completely new way of being in the world. Some of us are chomping at the bit.

I spent my life looking for a teacher, someone who could explain to me what it's all about and what I'm meant to be doing, until a few years ago when I realized (with some help) that I had to step into my own power, and take responsibility for my own experience of reality. If you find a teacher who can help you, that's great—and still, we all have to be willing to take individual responsibility, developing our own individual points of view and making our own choices. There is nothing in this modern world to stop us experiencing life in depth if that is what we want, as long as we are willing to move beyond the habitual and cultural limits that prevent us being fully ourselves and fully alive. I do not for a moment pretend that this book is a definitive guide on how to do that, but it may at least promote some discussion on the topic.

Because the true nature of reality is so far beyond anything that we can capture with the intellect, and we as human beings have spent many centuries content with a very shallow understanding of it, we have not developed words to discuss it—and when we start to use words, we quickly find that they don't reflect the depth we are looking for. I have occasionally changed spelling, such as writing the word *yourself* as *your self*, to encourage the reader to think about the concept of self. I often use the word *choice*, to say that you have chosen the reality you are experiencing. I mean that some part of you really wanted to experience it, but that *wanting* may have come from a very different perspective than the one that you are accustomed to. Therefore, you may think, "I certainly did not choose this, I would never choose this!" Various questions then arise: who is the *you* that chose it? And if that *you* really wants to experience something that another part of you finds unpleasant, what can be done? Or was this reality imposed on you, and if so by whom? How can we learn to assert the reality we want from this daily human perspective when that part of us seems to have minimal control over the greater picture? What is this concept of choice? We tend to think that if we chose something, then we can just as easily choose the opposite. Using my definition of the word, that is not true. We cannot choose something just to please someone else, only if we genuinely want it. See more on this in Chapter Eight.

Many of the concepts I am promoting in this book are difficult to grasp with the intellect. Let them float in your consciousness, trusting that you will understand what you need to for now. I have repeated some concepts several times, using different words to present slightly different aspects as an aid to understanding. In the end, this book may just provide one phrase that will help you out. Don't feel like you have to read the book from beginning to end; I encourage you to open it at random, and because nothing happens randomly, it will open at the page you need, and your eye will catch what you need at that moment in time.

When we start to realize what is *out there* (the vastness of being) we can become overwhelmed with the sensation of that vastness, realizing we know so little it's virtually nothing. Sometimes I'm so astounded with the vastness of it all that I am certain I know nothing. Yet within the knowing of nothing-ness, whether known by me or by anyone else, there is always a profound wisdom, which is available to all of us.

I tell the story of how this knowing came to me in Chapter Ten, so read that first if it's important to you. In the end, I can sum up my method in a few words: I allow the awareness to come to me, with some prodding from AMAG[1], a group of realized beings with whom I have studied for nearly twenty years; and I spend a lot of time alone in Nature. If you are reading this book, the chances are high that you can also allow this knowledge to come to you. Some of you will have the same reaction as I did when I got the information I've written about: *Oh! Now I get it!* And some of the people who are reading this book will just think I am spouting garbage. That's life on Planet Earth. A huge diversity of being is represented here, which is a wonderful thing.

---

[1] AMAG is the name used to represent a multi-dimensional, intergalactic group consciousness available since 1982 through spiritual mentor and trance medium Dayana Jon Patterson. See www.dayanajon.com.

4

Many people in this world love to make rules about reality so that everything appears to be clearly black or white (which it very rarely is). They want to tell other people what's what, making simplistic categorical statements about right and wrong and what we ought to be thinking and doing. Because the real truth is too complex to be grasped so easily, this leads to false and limited thinking, inevitably promoting lies, or at least half-truths. Even nowadays, individuality and original thinking are not generally encouraged, yet our changing world demands that each of us connect with what is true for us personally, rather than blindly accepting what we are offered. This ongoing search for truth is a vital undertaking, made more difficult by people who are invested in maintaining the old lies or making up new ones that keep us in a state of confusion.

To help get started on this path of truth, I have listed below a few of the more standard misconceptions about the nature of reality that I hear often, along with my responses. Some of these misconceptions are more recent; others are ancient. The kind of people who find these beliefs reassuring won't want to read this book. Those of us who are disturbed that they are accepted so widely without being questioned will welcome the opportunity to examine them. Some of them have been stated as law for centuries by religious zealots who in many situations held the power of life and death over anyone who dared to question them, so their effect is very pervasive, even to those of us who have rejected them on a conscious rational level. We need to be proactive in our personal search for truth: unless we deliberately replace commonly told lies with something else, they will continue to affect our subconscious understanding of reality. You may not agree with what I have written, but perhaps you will begin to formulate your own ideas and discuss them with others.

We are not spiritual, and we should be.

We are all beings of spirit, existing beyond any concept of time and space. So we are all spiritual beings, whether we like it or not. From that perspective (which I refer to as All-that-we-are), we create these human bodies, and personalities to go with them, in order to have the delightful experience of being in a limited physical form. Think of it as a game. Most games have rules, but rules can always change, and new versions of games are constantly evolving. These days many of us are making new sets of rules for ourselves. That is perfectly acceptable. All-that-we-are has neither *shoulds* nor *oughts*. That said, one of the key aspects to this particular game here on Planet Earth is that we have physical bodies. We are learning how to be in this world from the perspective of an embodied being.

If we were enlightened, we wouldn't suffer.

We might define suffering as a state of being stuck. It is possible to experience intense emotions—even ones normally considered negative—without suffering. It's a matter of learning how to let them pass quickly. We all experience all kinds of emotions (otherwise known as feelings), and the closer one is to a true understanding of the nature of reality, then the more one allows oneself to feel them, and then the quicker they pass. Suffering, as I have defined it, only arises when we try to stop a feeling. People mean quite different things by the word *enlightened*, but it could be applied to anyone who doesn't get stuck in feelings.

This is a terrible world and it's getting worse all the time.

Have you read any history? A hundred years ago atrocities were occurring all over the world, and they were even worse a hundred years before that, and a hundred years before that. There are certainly some atrocities happening still now, and our determined media is constantly searching them out to inform us. Personally, I experience the world as a much fairer, kinder, freer, safer, and more truthful place than when I was growing up, sixty years ago, and I am delighted. I meet more and more people who are waking up and choosing to live compassionately.

This is a world of duality and that makes everything difficult, and it's all an illusion anyway.

You will often hear Buddhists referring to this existence as an illusion, and many people therefore assume that it is not important, or it's not supposed to be important. On the contrary, whether you think of it as an illusion or not, it is both powerful and valuable to those of us who have chosen to be here (which includes everyone who *is* here). The fact that it is a planet of duality just defines some of the ways we experience life here.

Night and day, dark and light, winter and summer, war and peace, love and hate; we cannot have one without the other. They define each other. Being trapped in duality, therefore, will mean many ups and downs in life. There is nothing wrong with that, but life may be more pleasant when you learn to experience the kind of peace that exists outside of duality. I'm talking about something that has nothing to do with war. Peace, truth, beauty, love—outside of duality, those words mean the same thing. Bliss, Nirvana, One-ness, and Enlightenment—they are all an experience of peace that exists beyond duality. We have chosen to be born into a dualistic world, and now many of us are bringing the experience of one-ness here. We're learning how to exist within duality without being trapped by it.

True saints, saviors, and gurus sacrifice themselves to come back again and again in human form to help those of us who are trapped in ignorance.

Once again—we are all beings of light choosing different manifestations on this planet. I can assure you that Jesus, Buddha, and Mohammed all led many lives in other human forms, and plenty of them were not pretty. From the perspective of All-that-we-are, nothing and nobody needs rescuing. Lives pass. Life is forever and always. The choice to manifest in human form is never a sacrifice. This world is one huge playground of life. If things get seriously out of balance, it is a simple thing for this planet to stop what is going on by destroying the relevant civilizations, and starting again. That has already happened many times in the history of the Earth. It's a natural cycle.

If we're not happy, we must be doing something wrong.

In the broad perspective from which we make choices, we don't intend to be happy all the time and it is impossible to do anything wrong. We can prolong an experience of suffering by choice, or by default, which means lack of choice—in other words, being stuck in suffering usually results from lack of understanding of how to change it. There's nothing wrong with that, and it certainly doesn't mean we are bad people. We just are in a process of learning. One of the reasons I am writing this book is to help people to understand how to stop suffering, but I know that some people will continue to suffer.

There is an energy source outside of ourselves (often called God) that is constantly judging us, and if we don't do things right, it will surely catch up with us and condemn us to a future life of misery. So watch out, because your karma will always come to get you!

There is nothing and no one to judge us except ourselves, All-that-we-are. In any particular lifetime we may feel that we have done something that goes against the intentions we have set for ourselves, and we may give ourselves a really hard time because of that. The intentions we set for ourselves vary enormously from individual to individual and from life to life. One person may experience tremendous remorse because she told a lie, when she had set the intention of being absolutely truthful in this life. Another person might tell lies all her life without suffering any remorse, because she didn't make any commitment to being truthful. What is common to all of us is a deep desire to experience both sides of the coin of duality. Having been the perpetrator in an abusive situation in one life, we will most certainly choose to be a victim in another life, and vice versa. It's not a punishment; from the perspective of All-that-we-are, neither is worse than the other. And when you choose to wake up (which means, to perceive the nature of reality from a broader perspective), you will look back on them *both* with compassion. *You* choose those experiences. *You* want them. The question is not how to avoid such lives, it is, "Who are *you*? Who or what is choosing these experiences?"

The ego is universally bad, keeping us trapped in a sense of self that will always prevent us from being truly fulfilled.

A great deal of nonsense is talked about the ego. We chose to be born here with this ego, and this character that goes with it. A necessary part of the game is differentiating into individuals, apparently separate. In order to be in human form, we must have enough of a sense of self and its attendant personality to develop our own ideas, and not be carried along in the masses. *I* must have a strong enough sense of *myself* that *I* can feel what is right or wrong for *me*. That sense of right or wrong varies widely from person to person. Just because something is wrong for me doesn't mean it is wrong for someone else. If I don't have enough of a sense of myself, how do I decide what's right? Do I just believe what others tell me? Plenty of people operate that way right now, and if they are soldiers in the army, they kill other people when they are told to do so. I personally find that alarming and unfortunate. Doing things to glorify one's image as perceived by others is different. See Chapter Six.

If we aren't succeeding in choosing joy, we are not trying hard enough.

Trying is often the problem. Making an effort to do something is like swimming towards something we want. The agitation of the water created by our movement actually pushes it away from us. As we perceive what we want nearby, we need to learn to be still, to allow the current to bring it to us. Being still is an art and I will write more on it later.

If we knew what the future held, we would be able to avoid the bad things.

Think of life like a game of football. If you always knew who was going to win, who was going to score the goals, and exactly how many goals, it would spoil the game. As the fully evolved beings of spirit that we truly are, we know everything that is going to happen. We've intentionally set this life up so that we forget that knowing. We've forgotten who and what we are. That is an amazing thing, and it makes for a remarkable play. OK, sometimes people get unpleasant injuries in football. Sometimes a team gets on a losing streak. But people still play. A lot of people still play, and they love it.

We must struggle against evil.

What you resist persists. What you focus on is what you get. If you fight against something, you are putting energy into it, and unless there are some other influences at work, it will get stronger as you become more and more embroiled in it. You may get stronger too, or you may get very tired. Struggling is a choice. Most of us get tired of it after a while. Stepping back and getting a broader perspective is part of the art of being human. You can't create peace through struggle. You may be able to create a temporary improvement, but it won't last. If you want to stop fighting, then stop fighting.

Desire (especially sexual desire) is a lowly emotion and truly spiritual people are not bothered by it. They feel calm and happy all the time.

If we want to experience life fully (and that is usually what we came into the world to do), we need to learn to allow the sensation of desire to course through our bodies. Our physical bodies are incredible vessels, and when we allow them to feel fully, and let go of any emotion that we have been storing from the past, we find that they inform us of everything we need to know. Knowing becomes a body sensation, not something isolated in the rational brain (a phrase I am using to include the workings of the intellect and the mental thought processes, which are useful tools, but limited ones). Allowing ourselves to feel desire is what enables us to make changes in our lives. Constant outward calmness is often a sign of someone who has quelled the experience of emotion. There is nothing wrong with that, but such people will most certainly want to live other lives where they allow themselves to feel their feelings fully. Personally I enjoy people who are enthusiastic and energetic. Sexual desire, and orgasm in particular, is one of the quickest ways for a human to have an experience of bliss. That's why so many religions preach against it: some people don't want you to find out that it's easy to have an orgasmic life. I have included a chapter on sex in this book because we need to start talking about it and learning what it has to teach us.

The Day of Judgment is about to arrive, the world is coming to an end, and we had better hurry up and get our shit together.

Many of us are concerned about the state of the world, especially as we keep hearing prophecies from various sources about its end. A lot of people are afraid. While that's understandable, it's important to realize that we can't change what is happening on a global scale, we can only change our own attitudes to it. I personally am excited and delighted about the future of this world. I feel we are moving into a positive phase of evolution, where our currency will be compassion rather than money. It may be true that there will be lots of natural disasters. Maybe I will die in one. Maybe I won't. Whichever of those is to happen, I can be sure that I will be in the right place at the right time, so that what is *right* will manifest. I'm sure of that because I know that nothing is accidental or incidental. I'm certainly not going to waste my time trying to avoid the *right* destiny. That is a ludicrous concept. In any case, dying is a fine thing to do, and we all do it.

All spiritual people are good.

There is a regrettably common assumption that human beings who are clearly spiritually inclined and any beings who are not in physical form must all be innately good, except perhaps for a few who are clearly demonic. I've already explained that we are all spiritual people. Being good or not has nothing to do with how aware we may be of our spiritual origins. It is very possible for a spiritually powerful person (that is, someone who can communicate and work with unseen energies) to be completely lacking in integrity. As for beings who are not currently in any physical form—they are just like those of us in human form: some are bad, some are good, some are stupid, some are wise, and there is a great span in between.

We are the only sentient, intelligent beings in this Universe.

Quantum physicists are seriously questioning this kind of limited thinking and, as we humans graduate from kindergarten, people are beginning to accept that there is a great deal more going on around us than meets the eye. We are surrounded by unseen beings. Some are not a whole lot more advanced than us, and some don't have the best intentions. Some are sages and crones, tuned into depths of wisdom and knowledge that are light years beyond our comprehension. For whatever reason, many of them are interested in this planet and are happy to offer us help.

11

More on how to access that help and why we can't see these beings later.

If you really want to believe something, then it is suspect and you definitely should not believe it.

My brother told me this when we were talking about life after death. He's a lawyer, with a world-view very different from mine. If a thought or a concept intrigues you, my advice is to investigate it. There is probably some kind of truth there for you, even if it's not what's immediately apparent on the surface. You might decide to believe it just for fun, or just because you want to. There is no need to stick with beliefs that can be grasped by the rational brain and proved by scientific means. That's very limiting. What harm can it do to try out a new and different belief? You are in charge of your own life and you can always change your mind.

If we are truly compassionate and good people then we will spend all our time working to alleviate other people's suffering.

People need to go through what they need to go through, and it is not anyone's job to stop the process. We won't be doing them any favors if we do try to stop a process that needs to carry on to completion, and we won't succeed anyway. Helping others often stems from an egotistical need to be seen as a good person. This is one case where the ego should be thrown out of the window. *Good* can be an unhelpful label that motivates us to do things because we need other people's approval, rather than because we really want to do them. The best thing we can do for the world is whatever brings us joy, because joy is infectious.

Chapter Two

Who and What

"You are the Sun in drag.
You are God hiding from yourself." [2]

Whether we are seeking more depth, or just looking at how to improve our lives, the most profound question anyone can ask is not, *How do I choose joy*, but rather, *Who am I? Who is doing the choosing? Who or what created this body with this personality, and why?* Acknowledging our alignment with the *I* that chose this body and infuses life into it makes everything unfold more smoothly and enables us to pass on quickly from experiences we find unpleasant.

So, what are we then?

In short, we are consciousness choosing human form. Because the consciousness that we are exists in an awareness of reality radically different from human awareness, it is beyond the ability of the rational brain to grasp, and we don't really have words to describe it, although we might choose a word like *magnificent* or *vast*. What we truly are is vast beyond anything we can grasp from our limited human perspective, and when we first allow even a limited awareness of that, it may be quite frightening. We could also be described more simply as beings of light and sound. We have no form except when we decide to manifest. We can do that many, many times in many different forms. Why would we want to? Because it's interesting and fun to have a limited form when you are completely accustomed to being formless and unlimited.

---

[2] Hafiz, in *Love Poems from God: Twelve Sacred Voices from the East and West* by Daniel Ladinsky (Compass, 2002).

From the perspective of formlessness, things look very different. A friend once asked me, why is it that answers to spiritual questions are always confusing and hard to understand? Why do great truths always seem to be shrouded in mystery? The answer is because they are hard to comprehend from our narrow human perspective. Seeing things from a very broad perspective is a useful practice. You may think of it as stepping backwards or dropping downwards. From that place, things like cars breaking down, feeling unappreciated, fearing you're going to be late for an appointment, and so on, are quite unimportant. We can also meet larger things, such as death, with equanimity when we are able to choose a vaster perspective.

But even the deepest perspective a human could adopt cannot reveal the true state of the Universe; it is far too great for us to conceptualize. We can only make vague approximations. The ultimate Truth of existence will always be a mystery to us, and that's fine.

Why is it so frightening to know ourselves as vast? Accepting that we are so powerful completely transcends ego, and to the ego, that feels like dying. Within human existence, we are accustomed to a sense of smallness and to being at the mercy of the world around us. We are used to being able to compute things with the rational brain, which is immediately overwhelmed when presented with the vastness of the Universe. More than anything, when you know you are infinitely powerful, you must take responsibility for yourself. You can no longer blame something being out of your control when you know that to say you are out of control is a lie. Being presented with that reality can be earthshaking. Marianne Williamson says, "Our deepest fear is that we are powerful beyond measure."[3] She's right.

Play the game and don't take it so seriously

Human life is a game. We set life up so that we are unaware of the immensity that we really are, because we couldn't play the game in the same way otherwise. The fact that we don't remember who and what we really are make this game deeply engaging. So if you don't

---

[3] Marianne Williamson, *A Return to Love: Reflections on the Principles of "A Course in Miracles."*

feel like an eternal, all-powerful being, you're doing fine—that's the way it's meant to be.

All games get boring eventually. And then, you change some of the rules to make it engaging in some other way. That's what we are doing as we wake up and get inklings of the truth. Only those of us who have played many times, over and over, are willing to wake up, and those of us in that situation are changing the game of life for ourselves.

Just because existence is a magnificent mystery doesn't mean we have to go around trembling with awe. We already tend to take it far too seriously. *It's a life or death situation* is a phrase we all know, as though dying is the worst thing that can happen, and must be avoided at all costs. Longevity and quality are usually unrelated. Die young or die old—it really doesn't matter in the long run. Death is an absolutely essential aspect of being human. Imagine how carelessly we might live if we knew we could never die.

I don't want to belittle the grief that often accompanies the death of a loved one. I encourage you to allow yourself to feel that grief fully when it arises. But this society is phobic about death (and sex—the two things we think we cannot control), and that is unhealthy. Do you want your family and friends to dread your death and avoid it in every way they can, or simply to honor it when it occurs? Do you want them to celebrate everything you have given them and be grateful for the time they have had with you? When someone dies, the qualities that they have personified become available for others to integrate into their lives. Death opens doors. It may force us to feel things we have worked hard to avoid. It may break our hearts wide open. No life is ever wasted—that is an impossible concept.

Life is always. We weren't meant to get it right the first time, and there is no such thing as getting it right anyway, because there is no one judging. We can choose again and again and again, forever and ever and ever. There are no limits. Play. Enjoy. Laugh. Experiment. Live. Die. Live again.

Planet Earth is a playground, not a school. Truthfully, mistakes are impossible. Many people think that our only purpose in being human is to learn. Although we *will* learn a great deal being in human form, the primary reason we chose to be here is to enjoy the game.

Like football, it's sometimes hard work, and the longer we play it, the more we understand the nuances of it. If you are going to partake in this particular game here on this planet, you must abide by at least some of the rules, which include forgetting who you really are. If you break that rule on a consistent basis, you will be playing quite a different game. It may be so different that you find life on this plane intolerable.

Other lives

Most of us have heard of the concept of past lives. That phrase is misleading, since they don't all occur in the past. They are created from a perspective that is beyond time, where past, present, and future are meaningless terms—but since the concept of time is essential to human experience, we can't imagine what it would be like to exist without it. We just have to accept (or not, if it feels wrong to you) that the vastness that we truly are is manifesting in many different bodies, with many different personalities, in many different places and times. We are consciously choosing all of them and infusing life into them, and when we create them we have a pretty good idea what kind of life scenarios we are expecting for each of them, although things can always change. It's fascinating to think how the individual lives unfold in this state of complete forgetfulness that enables us to believe our stories and allows the game to be played with ferocious intensity.

If you're doing all these things, living all these other lives, how come you are not aware of them? Your physical form would be overwhelmed trying to grasp everything. Your rational brain would blow a fuse. Here's one metaphor that may help to understand it, using your whole body to signify All-that-you-are, and the different parts of your body to signify your different human lives: when you pick up a glass with your hand, you can think of it as your hand picking up the glass and you can also think of it as you picking up the glass. Some parts of your body have no awareness that you picked up the glass, and aren't apparently involved in the act of picking it up at all. Still, you picked up the glass. Or, your hand picked up the glass. Your hand knows exactly how to close its fingers around the glass, but your stomach, your toes, your tongue, none of them need to know anything about it. A knee is intending to be a knee, and things would get pretty silly if it was trying to do what a hand does, or worse still, trying to take over the job of the whole.

You might think of it as a movie. You went to one of those big theaters where they have a bunch of different movies playing. In this theater there are thousands of choices. You chose one that seemed interesting, but perhaps in the middle you decided you didn't like it. After all, this is the kind of movie you don't just watch—you are living in it. So, while it could be a great outlet for your need for drama to *watch* a horror movie, *living* in it would be entirely different. You might stay till the end because it has you gripped in some way, or you might leave that one and choose another. Different people like different kinds of movies. You often can't know what you like until you've tried a lot of different ones.

It has also been described to me as akin to a puppet show. You are the puppeteer and the puppet maker, and you also write the show in which the puppets play. You design everything about the show, down to what clothes the puppets are wearing. But don't make the mistake of thinking that you in this body are as powerless as a puppet. You in this body have an unbreakable and powerful relationship with the puppeteer, and many channels of communication are open between you. Once you begin to talk with yourself, you will constantly be exchanging information with yourself, developing new insights, and seeing new choices. You are doing that now, but when you are very conscious about it, everything speeds up and you are more able to choose a perspective that is pleasing.

Because this life is the one you are intending to lead, it's absolutely right that you are focused in the here and now, in this body, unaware of other lives you are leading. Occasionally, however, recalling another lifetime can help you in the here and now. You may be able to do that by setting your intention and then creating a space to do it, or you may find a practitioner who can help you.

Beyond comparison and counting

We often hear references to the terms, *higher self* or *higher power*. I am leery of these phrases as they smack of separation and hierarchy. In truth, there is no one state of being that is better than another. Would you say your hand is better than your foot? Is your hand better than your whole body? Do you think your liver is better than your heart? All-that-you-are that is eternal, all knowing, and exists outside of time is *who you are*. In this experience of that consciousness that you are, there is nothing less or more, nothing negative or positive, nothing bad or good. Those concepts do not exist because there is no limitation of any kind, anything and many things we can't imagine are available to us, and time is an utterly meaningless concept. There is only everything. No one manifestation is any better than another.

The word *soul* is also questionable because it implies that it's something you are separate from when you refer to *my* soul. Even the term All-that-you-are is a little misleading because it indicates that it is possible to be less-than-you-are. It is really more truthful to call yourself what you are: a consciousness choosing human form. *You* are consciousness choosing human form. You could have chosen, and may in fact be choosing, a form other than human. There are plenty of different ways to experience physicality, and at this point in our evolution we humans know very little about the variations.

The concept of the Universe (as in, *the Universe will provide*) can be useful—as long as you remember that we all created the Universe. We *are* the Universe. The word *God* is tricky because it gives many people an image of a man with a long white beard sitting in the clouds watching us. The word *Goddess* can be useful but only in a limited context since the consciousness that we are does not relate to gender. That delightful and fascinating male/female thing is an aspect of duality.

Truth and illusion

Understanding who we are involves understanding Truth, which is a vast concept. There is a huge difference between personal truth and universal Truth. The former is about one's personal perception. We all perceive things from our own perspective, which means from the position that we are occupying, and since no two people can occupy exactly the same position, everyone's perspective is absolutely unique.

Universal Truth is about what actually exists. For instance, it is the Truth that we are all beings of light (insofar as words can convey that). According to that level of Truth, this planet and all other physical manifestations are an illusion. They are not real. Nevertheless, it is vital to understand that they can still affect us powerfully, because we experience them as real. That's the way it's meant to be. Yes, this Earth is an illusion. It is an incredible, marvelous, beautiful illusion. Just because it's an illusion does not detract from its magnificence at all. It still affects and moves us very deeply. The skill of being human is *not* about preventing ourselves from being moved; it is about allowing that movement absolutely freely. In other words, we are intending to feel all our feelings rather than avoid them. See Chapter Seven.

Wisdom and the rational brain

People who are using the rational brain to try to comprehend this kind of stuff want proof. It can't be done. What I am talking about is far too great to be measured. There are no known scientific methods to test anything I am saying, although some people do enjoy trying, and there is nothing wrong with that—it's just a way to play the game. If you don't believe in life after death or anything else I'm saying, that's fine. If you find yourself intrigued by what I am saying, perhaps you want to investigate it further. I would suggest that you investigate how it feels in your body. True knowledge is a sensation. Information is what the brain deals with. A quick brain makes you clever but it can never make you wise. Allowing energy to flow through you and recognizing the sensation of truth is what makes you wise. That is how to know right from wrong. It's a personal thing. You can practice this by saying out loud: *My name is (whatever your name is)*, and follow it with, *My name is (something it's not)*. When you are using a name that vibrates at a different frequency from the frequency at which you yourself are vibrating, then it will feel uncomfortable. See Chapter Three for more information on vibrations and feelings.

Science can be an interesting study, and I am not discouraging it. However, it is limited because a huge percentage of what is going on in our cosmos cannot be comprehended or measured by present scientific methods on this planet. We are beginning to see some eminent scientists who are very disillusioned with science. Dr. William Tiller, a Stanford researcher in his seventies, recently did a series of experiments proving that the outcome of an experiment, no matter how carefully controlled, is affected by the intention (or

19

motivation, or desire) of the people in charge of it. He claims that a human being's intention is "capable of significantly affecting both the properties of materials (non-living and living) and what we call 'physical reality.'"[4] In other words, if someone is conducting an experiment with the intention of proving something, they will probably be successful. If someone else conducts an experiment with the intention of *disproving* the same thing, they will probably be successful, even if both experiments are considered scientifically sound. We create our own reality, or at least, we create our own perceptions of reality, and we can change those or reinforce them with the power of our intentions. Many of the so-called laws of physics are not really laws at all—they are concepts that may be useful for a while in the evolution of our planet. We are beginning to find out that not everyone *has* to abide by them, and it would be smart to let those concepts change over time, as we ourselves change over time.

A few people have suggested to me that developing an awareness of our vastness might feed the ego in an undesirable way. In fact, this doesn't happen, because when the ego gets a glimpse of our true place in the cosmos, it immediately perceives it has no control and gets very scared—which is why some people really don't want to know what I am saying here.

In this chapter I have said little beyond the fact that we are magnificent beings, and we deliberately forget that in order to play the game of being human. Why, then, even bring it up? It makes a big difference to have that awareness to fall back on. When you are at the end of your tether, you've tried everything, and nothing helps, you might as well relax into the arms of All-that-you-are. Indeed, however you think of that (and I encourage you to phrase it in a way that feels right to you), handing over control to something greater than your rational brain is the basis of the art of being human. After all, entrusting even a tiny aspect of the orchestration of the Universe to the rational brain is a sure recipe for stress. In the end, human existence is all about relaxing and trusting in that *something greater* instead of gritting your teeth and forcing a particular outcome.

---

[4] From Dr. William Tiller's website, www.tiller.org. See William Tiller in the appendix.

Chapter Three

Everything is Energy

"The boldness of asking deep questions may require
unforeseen flexibility if we are to accept the answers." [5]

Before going any further with esoteric discussions about the nature
of reality, I want to bring some of these notions into the arena of the
concrete reality that we manifest in every moment of our existence—
what we call daily life. We can deliberately shape our reality by
learning to work and play with the consciousness-that-we-are. We
have to be fully alive, allowing that energy of the life force that we are
to move through us freely. This is what I mean when I talk about the
art of being human.

Energy—the stuff of everything

Everything is energy. What we see in physical form is merely energy
vibrating slowly enough that it has become dense and is therefore
visible to us; or more truthfully, because we have agreed to see it. We
can most easily affect what is manifested in physical form before it
becomes physical—when it is still energy invisible to us. It's vibrating
faster then and is more malleable. Like anything else that we're not
used to doing, deliberate shaping of energy requires practice,
although we have all been doing it without realizing what we were
doing. You can't exist in physical form without constantly
manifesting things, which simply means shaping energy. We all have
our explanations of how things come to us, but really, those are just
stories we tell. If it came to you, then you manifested it, whether it is
invisible or as real as a plate of food and the body you inhabit.

---

[5] Brian Greene, a Columbia University physics professor and author of *The
Fabric of the Cosmos: Space, Time, and the Texture of Reality.*

One of the easiest ways for most of us to learn how to recognize flows of energy is through sexual desire and arousal. Sex is a very powerful flow of energy that many of us are familiar with. See Chapter Four.

Energy vibrates at different frequencies. We all know the vibration of sound, which is just one form of energy. Everyone who knows anything about music knows that some sounds don't go together. They are unpleasant when they are combined. Others flow together well. This has to do with how their frequencies mesh or don't mesh. All energy has its own frequency. Some sounds, some people, some places, some events just don't feel comfortable to us. We can find all kinds of reasons why that is. In the end, it's because the frequency of those sounds, people, places, or events doesn't mesh with the frequency of the energy that we are.

Vibration and integration of truth

You may be in the habit of being around energy that doesn't match your frequency, and you are so familiar with the resulting jarring sensation that you don't notice it much. The art of being human is about really paying attention. As you practice, you will become aware of discomfort and you will know what needs to be changed.

When I first started questioning the nature of reality, I would sometimes experience goose bumps or a physical shudder. After a while, I figured out that this was a physical reaction to what was occurring around me. Someone had said something, or I read something, or I saw something, or I suddenly understood something that was reflecting Truth. The shudder was an adjustment in my own personal energy field (or auric field) to integrate this new awareness. Sometimes I feel the need to shudder when I am thinking about something profound. The need to stretch or yawn is similar. It allows the energy that makes up the physical body to re-align itself so that it can manifest—or reflect or integrate—a greater understanding.

A number of people are in the habit of using names that are not in synchronicity with who they are. If you have an inkling that you want to change your name, then give it a go, and see if another name feels more comfortable. Using the correct name can have remarkable long-term benefits—you may feel more relaxed, and things will happen more easily for you because your energy is flowing more smoothly.

The power of thought

Thoughts are a form of energy that quickly and easily manifest into physical form. Everything that we experience and everything we see around us was first thought by someone. It might not have been specifically your thought. It might have been a collective subconscious belief, or a thought by a being of spirit rather than a being in physical form. A belief is a thought that we have accepted so deeply we don't think about it anymore. Although there is a thin line between them, thinking about something is different from thinking something. When we think something, and don't contradict the thought, it becomes a desire, and as that feeling of desire floods our being, then what we have thought will manifest. Thinking about something is more a state of wondering if we want that something to manifest. See more on this in Chapters Seven and Eight.

Bringing everything to the surface

We often confuse ourselves and stymie the process of manifestation by contradicting a thought. That occurs in many ways. Most commonly, we already have some kind of belief system that is in conflict with the thought. We may be unaware of the conflict, or we may not *want* to know about it, or we think that if we ignore it, we can override it. Sometimes we can. But perfecting the art of being human requires being continually, deliberately, and carefully introspective, rather than leaving things to chance. It's necessary to change those old habits of glossing over what's difficult or quickly ignoring any thoughts that might challenge our image of ourselves as good, smart, clever, bold people (these are just my words—insert whatever adjective applies to your image of yourself). We need to start looking at what we are *really* thinking and feeling. We need to get in touch with our true motivations and let go of any judgments we might have about good and bad, any *oughts* and *shoulds* that are preventing us from acknowledging the truth. We're not trying to change these old habits because we think we ought to. We're looking at them to see how they may be helping or hindering our ability to live fully.

There is a spectrum here: at one end, absolute personal power, which is always a place of trust and truth, and at the other, serious denial, which means being full of inner conflicts that are not addressed, and therefore living a life of falsehood. Most people exist somewhere in the middle of this spectrum. There is nothing wrong with being in denial. Many of us are in denial a little, and a lot of people may be able exist happily that way. It's just that if you are refusing to be truthful with yourself, you will always be using some of your energy to maintain the lie, and the lie will prevent you being a clear vessel. You will inevitably be trying to block the flow of energy through you to some degree.

So I'm recommending that you learn to be absolutely honest with yourself, which means developing the ability to separate yourself and sit to one side, watching your mind, watching how you react, watching what feelings come up. When you notice a feeling that isn't synchronous with what you want, you need to decide what is more important to you. For instance, although you want a fancy new car, you may feel that it doesn't jive with your ideas of being environmentally aware. You need to examine if you really think that owning a vehicle like that does mean you are not concerned about the environment, and if so, do you want to change that belief? Perhaps you are denying yourself the fancy car because you think it might be damaging to the environment, and consequently there is a part of you that feels angry with and judgmental of people who do have fancy cars. That kind of self-righteousness will tend to make you treat people unkindly. Is that OK with you?

I can't tell you what conclusion to reach on this issue (or any other), but I can tell you that being determinedly attached to certain specific ideas of right and wrong often has negative effects, and denying yourself things that you want often leads to resentment. The classic example of this is a couple who resent each other because they have stayed together when they really wanted to part. Overlooking your own needs on behalf of a relationship is a common dynamic in many families, and it's culturally encouraged. It can manifest in many ways: perhaps you made an unspoken commitment to live near your parents years previously, and you feel like you are betraying them when you want to move. Perhaps you are still taking care of your adult son because he appears unable to take care of himself and you feel responsible for him. These sorts of behavioral habits have often been going on for years and require radical solutions. You have to decide on your priorities. Do you really want to change those old ways of being that are contributing to a shallow and unsatisfying existence? In truth, no one benefits from those familial patterns. You can choose to change them.

Such dilemmas are fairly common when you start to make changes and therefore choose to be honest, but they aren't always as hard as the ones I've mentioned above. You can practice with easier ones, and get help with the difficult ones. An important part of a therapist's job is to help you to move on from old patterns that are getting in the way of living your life fully. A good therapist can be a wonderful boon. However, if you are interested in the concepts I am discussing here, you must find someone who can work with the unconscious rather than someone who wants to talk things through on the rational level, since most of our deep-seated beliefs are not accessible on a rational level. Many of our fears are body memories that can be accessed and changed through bodywork. A good body-worker knows this and can help you to release blocks.

If you want to manifest something more unusual, such as the ability to levitate, you will need to enter or create a matrix of belief systems outside the norm. See Chapter Eight.

Other blocks

Sometimes what stops us manifesting particular things is a decision we made before we were in this particular physical form. For instance, you (as a consciousness) may have decided that you want to experience poverty in this lifetime. Remember, the perspective from which you choose to manifest as human does not grasp concepts of pain or pleasure. Although you can always change your mind about what you experience in this particular life. See Chapter Eight on more specific pointers about how to change your choices. The fact is that if you want to experience poverty, then you *will* experience it in some life or other. The good thing is that much of what we initially assume will be unpleasant doesn't in fact have to be so, and that includes poverty. The most useful way to approach this is to experience poverty fully, rather than railing against it. What we resist persists. You might find it's a delightful opportunity to examine all kinds of things: the relationship of money to happiness, the attitudes of rich people to poor people and vice versa, for instance. Those are just a couple of many possibilities.

Experiencing something fully, which means feeling it fully and being one hundred percent present for it, allows it to change. Most of us are very cautious about letting ourselves be flooded with sensation, which is what's required. This is true even of the experiences we consider good; we are afraid we will be bowled over by them. However, when we allow a sensation to fill us up so that we feel it in every cell of our bodies, we will finish with it quickly, whereas if we try to stop feeling it, then it will hang around waiting to be felt. Blocking flows of energy is a common human habit, and one I will be referring to in later chapters.

You may have to deal with feelings from another lifetime. Phobias and intense emotional responses with no apparent basis are often residues of other lives, waiting for resolution. These days there are a number of qualified healers who can take you on guided visualizations to access other lives and deal with those issues.

If all this internal examination is too difficult, you may still be able to live a full and satisfying life. It depends if you have hidden conflicts, and how deep they go.

Our ability to reason and remember

I have said some negative things about the rational brain so let me extol its virtues. Without it, I could not have written this book and you could not be reading it. Our mental faculties enable us to establish habitual behaviors so that we don't have to learn everything anew every day. Once we know how to walk, we can get out of bed every morning and walk without having to learn it all over again. We can learn all kinds of things and utilize them on a regular basis, enhancing our lives enormously as a result. Problems arise only when we give the rational brain too much power, when we try to rationalize ourselves out of a sense of discomfort or other emotions that are trying to get our attention, and when we use the brain to make judgments that it is not equipped to make—such as what is right and wrong, what is true or not. The rational brain is a tool, not intended to be in charge. Leave that to the heart or the gut.

Chapter Four

Sex and the Wisdom of the Body

"I am not the one who loves, it's love that seizes me." [6]

Most of my teaching is about getting people to drop away from speech and other mental processes into a deep place of power, which is often wordless. But when it comes to sex and death, which both take us to that glorious and terrifying place of power where we cannot hide, I encourage people to talk. Usually we shy away from talking about them, because the rational brain, which is what we use to form words, is frightened by the sense of being out control that such extremely powerful processes tend to inspire. We need to tap into that power, however it arises, and bring it into the everyday arena of the rational brain, giving it words; and we need to take our daily mundane run-of-the-mill rational processes, which are mostly far too wordy, into that deeper wordless place where we can see what is real and what is not.

Our society has tremendous misconceptions about sex; in what follows, I encourage you to forget everything you ever heard about what it is. Read as though you are an alien who has just come to Earth for the first time and has never before heard of sex.

Allowing desire

When we really want something, it becomes a desire, a physical sensation of wanting. When we allow that sensation to fill our bodies,

---

[6] Leonard Cohen, "You Have Loved Enough," from the album *Ten New Songs.*

we are halfway to getting it. That sense of excitement and delight that comes with imagining how we will feel when we get what we desire will bring the thing to us. This is all about allowing a flow of energy (which is in this case the experience of desiring something), and most people easily learn how to allow that from the experience of sexual desire and arousal. An orgasm, which is about allowing energy to flow through us freely, is ecstatic precisely because the free flow of energy through the body is an ecstatic sensation, *whatever causes it*— and it can only occur when we let go of any attempt to control the body. That is a profound piece of wisdom. When we can learn to trust the body on a daily basis, all kinds of possibilities open up, *not* just sexually.

Human beings have tried and tried and tried to pretend that their smaller selves are in control of their lives, which is why they have belittled the power of the body and glorified the power of the rational brain. It hasn't worked and cannot work, and that is most obvious in the arena of sexuality. No amount of rational thinking can prevent us being turned on by what turns us on, even if we decide not to act on it. We need to give up trying to stop it, acknowledging that the-vastness-we-truly-are is in control, and figure out instead how to live our lives with integrity, yet without denying what we are being required to experience. Life in human form is an experiment in consciousness, and nowhere is that more obvious than when it comes to sex. We hear more nonsense and outright lies about sex than anything else. Do yourself a favor: begin finding out *for yourself* what it is, what it has to offer *you*, and how *you* want to play with it.

Because sex is a source of power far beyond the realm of the rational brain is exactly why it has been put down so much by so many religions, at least the ones where power-over-others is invested in the hands of priests. Most earth-based spiritual practices revere sex as the ultimate source of creativity and truth, as a form of worship in itself. Clearly, sex can be a very powerful healing force: restorative, clearing, expansive, and profound. Because we live within duality, sex can be used to do the opposite of healing: to alienate, destroy, pervert, and hurt people. It is a quick gateway to bliss, available to everyone, and a strong motivator that can do considerable damage in the hands of someone who doesn't have a commitment to behaving with respect for others. It can easily destroy or enhance a person's self-esteem, on deep levels, by making us feel powerful or powerless.

It can quickly and easily open doorways to realms far beyond the physical. We have a great deal to learn from sex about how to tap into energy flows for the benefit of all, extrapolating information that we can then use to create bliss in our daily lives.

The body

Sex cannot be separated from the fact of being in physical form: that is, having a body. The power of the body and our relationship to it are very important because the body gives us instant access to the wisdom of All-that-we-are, and it *never* lies. Our bodies are a field of energy that is an immediate reflection of what we are thinking. What we are thinking is what our minds are dwelling on. For instance, a lot of people spend a lot of time thinking about what they look like, and worrying that they don't look good enough. Since they generally consider beauty only skin-deep, they try to make themselves more beautiful by changing what is on the surface.

But what we are thinking about most is what we will manifest. So, if we spend a lot of time thinking about, reading about, and looking for fat, we are likely to manifest fatness. It doesn't matter that we don't want to be fat—if that's what we are focused on, it's going to manifest. This is a good example of how cultural fears affect us. It's a compelling reason to divorce ourselves from our cultural belief patterns—not an easy thing to do since an enormous number of people on Earth think in this limited and negative way.

Why some people get fat and not others is due to many factors: for instance, what kind of life they intended to lead before they were born, and other influences around them to which they are susceptible—or not.

Develop an ongoing two-way relationship with your body. It's your friend: you talk to it and it talks to you, just as you would chat with any friend. You are both interested in helping each other to be happy. You can think of your body as the temple that you have to live in this lifetime. It's also a source of great wisdom, and when we stop bullying it or forcing it to conform to the specifications of the rational brain, we will find that it is very pliable. It wants to please us. It just can't do everything, and we often give it confusing messages. We look at a chocolate éclair and think, "Yum!" Just as our tastebuds are responding to this thought, we think, "Oh, that will be so bad for me! I'll never be able to digest all that sugar and cream, and my immune system will plummet! And I'll get fat!" Now your body doesn't know how to react. If you go ahead and eat it, without contradicting the belief that it will be bad for you, your body will indeed have trouble dealing with it.

You might think, "Oh, that will be so delicious, and I eat so little sugar and cream that it won't be any problem for my body. I could afford to eat ten of those with no negative effect. I'll just have one right now." Then you and your body will really be able to enjoy it, unless you are already being affected by a lifetime of confusion, which most of us are.

Just making the above statement and pushing away the thought that first arose—that the éclair was going to be bad for you—doesn't work. You have to be absolutely honest with yourself. Your rational brain may be able to deny the truth but your body knows. You have to go deep enough to change your beliefs instead of ignoring them and hoping for different results. The basis of good health is befriending and listening to your body, which always wants to communicate. You need to take the time to stop and listen to what it's saying. Since everyone is different, what it says will not always correspond to what the health "experts" say. You have to decide which you are going to believe—the external source or the internal source?

The chakras

The body is an energetic grid designed to create physical form that works in specific and extremely complex ways. The chakra system is a way of looking at energy centers in the body. Traditionally we are taught that there are seven chakras corresponding to different aspects of being in the world. Refer to the appendix at the back of this book to get more information on them. If you have a problem in a specific part of the body, the message you are being sent is probably to do with the closest chakra. For instance, if you have a problem in your throat, perhaps you are not expressing yourself well. This could apply to painting, dancing, and many aspects of self-expression other than speech. If you have a problem in the area of your heart, you may be required to examine how you give and receive love.

Sound healing is about using the vibration of sound to bring the body into balance, and it can be very valuable. Practice feeling the vibration of sound first in your throat, and then in any part of your body. Choose a sound that feels good to you. That vibration will help to loosen stuck stuff and get the energy moving. Tibetan singing bowls placed on or near the body can be effective in the same way.

A powerful orgasm rushing through the body can re-arrange the energy of the chakras, renewing and refreshing us, as well as sometimes leaving us with difficult emotions we have been trying to ignore, or with physical symptoms that remind us where we have blocks.

All systems are a way of defining and simplifying something so that we can study it, and consequently there is always much more to reality than any single system. There are other chakras in the body besides the seven we are normally taught, particularly in the area of the head and the hands. There are many chakras that don't lie within the body. Chakras can be seen as portals. A chakra is a subjective experience of a dimension. If that's a little too much for you, don't worry—you don't have to understand it.

Being kind to your body

We must learn to relax on a physical level. If there is only one thing that you learn from reading this book, let it be that. When you relax your body, when you let go of physical tension, when you stop holding yourself rigid, when you stop rushing around, you have stopped trying to block the flow of energy through you. Life will then be able to unfold naturally and flow through you with ease, which it wants to do. Everything will feel and look easier. That is what happens when you cease to resist the wisdom that comes from the being-that-is-you, that is infusing life into your body.

Sometimes we have been in a state of tension for so long that we have forgotten what it feels like to relax. Take some classes on relaxation techniques, read books, watch a video.

Some spiritual practices teach their students to sit in uncomfortable positions or go without sleep for long periods; on some Buddhist retreats, you are not supposed to brush your teeth. Although this kind of thing is changing to suit the demands of

Westerners, there is still a pervasive belief that the body is base and we must learn to ignore its needs, imposing our will upon it. Much Western medicine operates from this premise, treating the body as a machine that can be re-designed to operate correctly. This is not a useful or truthful perspective. The body is a conscious organism, constantly responding to unseen influences.

When you consistently override your bodily needs, your body will gradually deteriorate, which is what we have been taught to believe a body will do, as we grow older. In fact, that isn't necessary, but changing that reality requires a deep shift in our attitudes. It takes a serious commitment to learn how to treat the body with the gentle respect and attention that it needs in order to thrive over a period of many years.

Most people leave their bodies rather than listen to what they need. Literally, their consciousness may be yards away from the electrical field of the body, especially if they have had some unpleasant and painful experiences that they would prefer to avoid. Being in a body, which means being present for what is going on for you, will inevitably mean that you sometimes experience pain, both emotional and physical. Out-of-body experiences can be entertaining and educational. If that's what you want to do, then go ahead. However, doing that kind of thing repeatedly is antithetical to the art of being human, since occupying a human body, learning how to delight in that body and respect its needs, is an essential aspect to being fully human. Ultimately, this leads to a different and rewarding experience, and you can learn how to choose experiences that are pleasant rather than painful.

Bodies like to move. Be gentle and exercise every day (once a week is not enough). Do some kind of regular movement, whether it is stretching, yoga, dance, running, walking, or anything else that appeals to you. You want to remind yourself that you are in this body. Feel all your different muscles stretching and relaxing. Check in with your feet, with your knees, with your stomach, with all the parts of your body, allowing yourself to hear what it is they are saying today.

The issue of how much to exercise can be tricky. On the one hand, you don't want to push your body too hard. On the other hand, many Westerners are accustomed to sedentary lifestyles, which is not good for the body. Let's put it like this: if you cannot comfortably walk at least a mile or two a day up and down not-very-steep hills (unless you are disabled, of course), then your body is probably beginning to degenerate, and it needs some attention.

Sometimes giving your body attention is all it needs. Tell it you love it. Touch it and stroke it. Be kind to it. Eat what you enjoy and enjoy what you eat. Never eat anything just because you think you should, and don't eat out of anxiety. Face your anxiety and deal with it instead of stuffing it. Eat what your body wants. Rest when your body wants. Sleep when your body wants. Exercise when your body wants, in the way that your body wants.

Dancing, of all kinds, is a wonderful method of self-expression and it teaches you about rhythms. Life is a song that is inviting you to dance. Accept the invitation on every level. Good sex is an expression of love, and a body that has just had a delightful sexual experience is a happy body, glowing with life. Be grateful for that, and utilize it. Don't hold your body hostage. Don't rush it. Don't push it around. It's doing its best. Loving your body is part of loving your life, and there is nothing more important than bringing joy and love into everyday reality.

Sleep and illness

Deep sleep is a vital aspect of being human. When we're asleep, we process emotions, we integrate new experiences, and we refresh ourselves. That place between sleep and waking is a place of profound awareness, when we can bring all kinds of wisdom into our physical reality. Drowsiness is not a bad thing. However, if you find that you are frequently unable to stay awake when you really want to, you need to examine what is going on. Perhaps you want to avoid something: an external situation, an inner knowing, another person, life itself. Your body will tell you. Are you sleeping so that you don't have to listen to what your body is telling you?

Illness is not necessarily a bad thing. It has many causes. For instance, it may be a manifestation of inner (or outer) conflict, of the need to rest, or the need to change an external situation. If you hate your job, you could get sick so that you don't have to go to it. The consciousness that you are uses your body to get your attention, to get messages through to you. Don't jump to the conclusion that illness is an unfortunate problem, which must be fixed as quickly as possible. It may be telling you that you manifested in physical form for more important reasons than you have so far been focusing on. It may be telling you to rest. It may be telling you to wake up—even if you feel the need to sleep!

Getting sick may facilitate a change that you are ready to go through, one that requires changing old belief systems that have been embedded in the cells of your body. Many shamans and medicine people from indigenous tribes were expected to go through a period of sickness (called a shamanic break) before coming fully into their powers.

Your body is changing all the time. Everything passes, and things will pass faster if you do not resist them. Allow yourself to rest, allow your body to do what it needs; pay attention to the messages offered you by pain or discomfort. The body is a source of wisdom far beyond our limited rational thinking.

Sexual play

There is nothing wrong with being celibate. There is nothing wrong with being sexually active. They are just individual choices, and the fact that some people consider those who choose celibacy as more virtuous is a sad reflection on the people who think that. Of course, there are ways of being sexual with or without integrity and honesty, just are there are ways of doing anything in life with or without integrity and honesty. How you behave in any area is an individual choice. When it comes to sex, the consequences of acting without integrity are usually immediate, and in order to stay in denial about them (which both victims *and* perpetrators usually want to do), a person has to keep her/his consciousness very superficial, often by taking drugs or alcohol. Sexuality is such a quick way to experience power that it is very compelling, especially for people who don't have other creative outlets in their lives, or don't know of other ways to let energy flow through them. And because it is such a taboo area, people who have been damaged by rape or molestation often find it difficult to heal; they are usually discouraged from talking about what happened to them, and pain that must be kept secret tends to fester.

The use of sex as a way of establishing dominance is an old cultural pattern that is in the process of change, and in the new world paradigm, it won't be possible in the same way because individuals will not allow secrets of that kind, and treating people with respect will get a lot more kudos than establishing dominance. All of us can help to speed up that cultural change by being willing to talk openly about what used to be considered shameful and embarrassing.

Feelings of shame often arise in relation to sex. While shame is a function of the limited and judgmental perspectives that this society holds about sex and bodies, and therefore may simply fade as you move into a place where you define your own reality, such feelings are always telling us there is something we need to look at with a view to changing our lives. They always involve a need to be open and upfront about our needs and about our right to define our own needs. They may be telling us to change our circle of friends so that we can be around people who are able and willing to listen to us. They are about learning to develop a sense of ourselves and who we are in the world separate from what we have been told, knowing ourselves to be of value simply because of being who we are. Within duality, we might say that the opposite of shame is courage. Therefore, anyone who experiences shame can also experience courage. It requires a shift of perspective. I am not saying that is easy, but within the new paradigm there is support for that in a way that didn't previously exist.

Talking openly and without judgment about a subject is a sure antidote to any shame you may have attached to it. Women (and men) who don't enjoy sex much are often shy of broaching the subject because they think there is something wrong with them. Be sure, be very sure, there is nothing wrong with you. You are just being who you are. So be brave and talk anyway. You will be surprised at how many people are desperately grateful to meet someone who understands.

And men. When heterosexual men start talking with each other openly and honestly about sex and about their real needs and feelings, without blaming anyone else, we may be sure the world is changing for the better. Please be brave enough to do it soon. Preferably now.

Sex as a power game

Like life, sex is a game. It's about letting the body take control, trusting that it knows what it's doing. It's great fun to play when you don't take it too seriously, and when you find someone who enjoys the same rules as you, rather than doing it by some rote method, which is how you think it ought to be done. *Ought* and *should* have absolutely no place when it comes to sex. Being able to talk about the rules that you do want is vital, so you can make sure that you and your partner are playing by the same ones, and once you start talking with your partner you may be delighted at what unfolds. As I have already said, many of us are afraid of sex, because it destroys the illusion that the rational brain is in control. I have three words of advice about that: *get over it.* Form a partnership with your body, and work from there. If you find you are getting freaked out by what your body wants, then take a break and look really deeply at what is frightening you, with the intention of figuring out ways of giving your body what it wants without anyone getting hurt. Negotiate with your body and negotiate with your partner.

Because sex is such a powerful energy flow, it teaches us about power. It may be very important to you to be powerful in your daily life, but that doesn't mean you can't enjoy the experience of powerlessness in your sexual play. Or vice versa: you may find yourself frustrated with your lack of power in daily life, and you can relieve some of that frustration by establishing your power in the bedroom. That is the basis of domestic abuse, but playing with power in a sexual context (or any other context) does not have to be abusive; it *does* have to be clearly negotiated. That means you talk with your partners about what you want, without judgment, and agree on rules to play by. It requires knowing yourself and being able to listen to someone else. Those are skills that we can all benefit from, since they are essential components of living a truly compassionate life.

Power, energy, control—control, energy, power: it's all the same thing. When we make deliberate and honest choices, sex can be a playground where we experience all kinds of things we wouldn't want or don't have in our daily lives. The conscious experience of powerlessness in sexual play can make us *more* powerful in our daily lives—in fact, it is essential to learn about powerlessness if we want to learn how to be powerful in a real way. Consciously allowing

36

ourselves to be out of control in one arena of life can enhance the experience of being in control in other arenas. Sadly, being out of control by default, a common reality for women especially, often occurs because we are not brave enough to speak up about what we really need and want. That is not being friends with yourself; it is a betrayal of yourself. So be brave. Take the risk of speaking up for yourself.

Like all games, you can get really into it and take it to all kinds of places. Did you really enjoy playing hide-and-seek, or some other game, when you were a kid? Remember how important it was to find a really good place to hide, how excited you were when you caught someone, how you didn't want to stop for lunch? Sex is a grown-up game. Get really into playing it, find new ways of doing it, get really excited when you think about it, do it all day long, do it differently, do it without having an idea of an end or a beginning, incorporate all aspects of your being into it. Don't hold yourself back from it. As long as you and your partner talk about it honestly, you can't do it wrong.

Don't have anyone to be sexual with? Doing it with yourself is a wonderful way to love your body. Still can't get into it? That is most commonly because you don't like your body and don't like the experience of being physical. There is nothing wrong with that either, but since you *are* in physical form, it would be good to learn to enjoy it. So start back there, in the sections earlier in this chapter, making friends with your body. Don't approach it with the idea that you will end up being sexual, because what matters most (by a long chalk) is your willingness to form a loving partnership with your body—and that may or may not result in feeling sexual.

You may not be able to enjoy sex if you are doing it with someone whose energy vibrates at a very different frequency from yours. We have a great deal of misplaced kudos attached to staying with the same partner forever in this culture. In truth, as long as you do it from a place of respect and integrity, changing partners is perfectly fine. Perhaps it's not necessary: you may be able to change the dynamic of established sexual exchanges by taking charge, or *not* taking charge, whichever is not your normal role. Either way requires the ability to talk to each other and listen to each other without judgment.

37

Are you a woman who doesn't have orgasms and you think you should? Think again—the definition of sexual enjoyment is different for everyone and does not have to include what is identified as an orgasm. Like life, sex is an ongoing process, and as you get to know your own body, always listening to it with respect, all kinds of options open up. An orgasm can be an overwhelming experience and your body may not be ready for it. When it is ready, you will have one—if you are willing to set the stage.

Sex as shamanic play

I use shamanic methods in my teaching because they are about learning how to shape energy and they are always experiential: that is, they are about tapping into physical wisdom, or body awareness. I consider sex to be a shamanic activity because it is about working, or rather, playing with energy. It's fair to define sex as a concentrated form of energy which, when we allow it to flow through us, feels really good. Another way to say this is that our bodies are concentrated energy, and when we allow the energy to flow just as it wants to, it gives rise to very pleasant sensations, whether sexual or otherwise.

Like water, energy flows in different ways: it may be fast and furious or slow and steady or anything in between. The fast and furious kind tends to alarm us, since it can indeed feel ferocious and animal-like. The release of the flow is about expression, about what is inside being externalized and coming into form. It can build up and then release suddenly, like a powerful orgasm, or it can release steadily and gradually, or it may be a flow without a build-up. Creativity means externalizing and manifesting something from an energy flow. People who are particularly creative have a lot of energy wanting to flow, and when they try to stop it, all kinds of mental health problems may result, such as bipolar disorder, or depression, which is about energy that is stagnating because it has nowhere to go. A great deal of being a well-adjusted member of society is about learning how to facilitate flows of energy through one's body or restraining the expression of the flow until such time as it is appropriate. There are good reasons why we don't have sex in public places. It's easy to alarm others as well as ourselves with an unrestrained release of energy, especially if it has been building for a while.

Sometimes people who want to be gentle and kind have trouble allowing their energy to flow freely because they are afraid it might hurt others. The present epidemic of depression in the West is a result of this. As the planet is shifting, more people are choosing to be kind to each other, and kindness is also culturally rewarded. It's great that people are treating each other better than they have in the past, but it's sad that anxiety about hurting others means we keep ourselves in a state of depression. We need to allow each other to be expressive, knowing that expression of feeling is about the person who's feeling what s/he is expressing. It's not about *you*, and doesn't need to be taken personally.

Sex not only teaches us how to allow energy to flow through our own bodies, it also teaches us how to play with and shape the energy that is flowing through another person's body. That is what we are doing when we make love to someone. Having sex with someone is about the art of touch, about learning to dance with another person, about learning to play another person's body as you would a musical instrument. The energy, whether it is flowing through another person's body or an instrument, is alive. It is life force. It knows how it wants to flow, and the person who is playing the instrument is the facilitator, who must be in tune with it, in tune with its frequency.

Of course, the energy of a person has the mind of the person through whom it flows to contend with as well as its own "mind!" Human beings tend to be motivated (or paralyzed) by fear of sickness and injury, by fear of rejection by culture, family, and partner, and, in Western culture at least, by fear of being a *bad* person and doing the *wrong* thing. All these fears can prevent you from allowing energy to flow through you freely. In order to allow that free flow, you must either be motivated by very strong desire which will override your fears (although perhaps leave you ridden with guilt, a useless emotion), or you must let go of the fears and move into trusting that the energy will not harm you or anyone else. Indeed, you must believe that allowing the energy to flow will be of benefit, and therefore it is OK to stop trying to control it.

Blocking an energy flow

So we see that the art of being in physical form can be summed up as allowing energy to flow through us and manifest in the ways we choose—coalesce into the kind of form we want, that is, whether a physical thing or an event or a particular state of mind (such as happiness). In other words, when we are really accomplished at allowing energy to flow, we choose something, and it happens. But, as I have said before, most of us become accustomed to blocking energy. Even when the attempt to block the flow is producing uncomfortable pains and illnesses that Western medicine struggles to diagnose, we still do it because it is familiar. We don't know how to do otherwise. Do you remember being told, "Now, don't get carried away!" by your parents or friends? Yet that is exactly what a powerful energy flow does. It carries us away out of our staid, limited, rational personas, into a reality that, once we're used to it and have stopped trying to resist it, is blissful, delightful, and very much removed from the average daily life.

We need to realize that it is our fear of the flow, not the flow itself, which causes discomfort. Sex is a metaphor for life. Becoming adept in the art of being alive is about letting life flow through us, about allowing a flow of energy and remaining relaxed, trusting that the outcome will be beneficial. This kind of allowing cannot be forced. It cannot be artificially induced in any way. It cannot exist in an atmosphere of lies. It is absolutely real, and we must be willing to be absolutely authentic to allow it to happen. That means, being exactly who we are, nothing less and nothing more.

Sex and love

Many of us, women especially, believe that sex is primarily about another person, and that really good sex is about an experience of one-ness, which might also be called love, with that other person. We tend to believe that the experience of one-ness is inextricably tied up with our partner. That can get us into a lot of trouble, since assigning the power of creating such a sensation to another person is always false. Any and every perception of reality is to do with the person who is doing the perceiving. You may be able to tune into a completely different experience of reality than the person you are standing or lying next to, and the fact that you feel a great deal of love (or one-ness) is a tribute to you. Love always flows from *inside*.

In Truth, love has little or nothing to do with finding a partner. Many of us are terrified of living out our lives alone; we equate feeling loved with having a partner, who, of course, loves us. Yet, what are we talking about when we use this word? Don't we more often mean compatibility and companionship? Those things, along with the ability to communicate clearly (both listening to your partner's words and speaking your own), are what make a relationship work on a daily basis; love does not. It's possible to love someone very deeply, and yet need to stay well away from that person because she or he is abusive. No amount of loving will change an abusive person until he or she is ready to change.

Love, when experienced as one-ness, is quite different from compatibility and companionship, and it has nothing to do with any other single person except insofar as someone else's presence may facilitate our feeling it. But the presence of another person is never *required* in order to feel love; another person (whether a guru, a lover, a relative, a teacher, a therapist, or a complete stranger) may simply help to open doors, or rather, point to doors that are already open. The ability to recognize an open door and then have the courage to walk through it are your own qualities. Such gifts may feel that they are out of your control, because the depth and breadth of awareness necessary in order to feel love is far beyond the capacity of the ordinary brain. When you are in love, you are in touch with some wisdom far deeper than the brain can match. And so, it feels greater than the *you* that is used to feeling small. We humans know ourselves to be tiny and vulnerable when we are not aware of the presence of All-that-we-truly-are. We develop an unhealthy ego in order to bolster ourselves out of that place, but when we are in touch with the vaster self that we really are, the ego falls away. It has no place any more. And then we understand what tremendous strength there is in vulnerability, which at its most basic, means the willingness to be truthful, to be simply who you are without pretense.

Love, hate, and one-ness

This is a world of duality: peace and war, summer and winter, good and bad, night and day. Seeing through the limits of the physical eyes and intellectual understanding, we always perceive a thing in relation to its opposite. Through that perception, love cannot occur unless there is also hatred, and good cannot occur unless there is also bad. Within what I am referring to as 'one-ness,' these opposites don't

41

occur. Within one-ness, or unity, it is possible to have an experience of love that has nothing to do with hatred. The following words come close to describing it: joy, delight, beauty, peace, bliss, and ecstasy. Once again, it's about free-flowing energy. There are a number of ways to get to that place of free flow, and an orgasm is one of them. Our tendency to fixate on the person we are with when we have that orgasm is not useful. If we can have that sensation with one person, we can have it with another, and we can have it when we are alone, and we can have it without touching our genitals— although the fact remains that many of us most easily experience it through an orgasm that is sexually induced. Caught up in our daily lives, we find those blissful moments very hard to recapture; in fact, they cannot be captured or contained in any way, only allowed. Few of us dwell in that place of allowing for more than a few moments, or think about it much at all. It would be beneficial to practice staying there.

Unconditional love

A lot of people have sex by rote, usually because they think they are supposed to enjoy doing it that way. If they don't enjoy it, they are unlikely to talk about it because they think there is something wrong with them, and because there is so little support for anyone who has conflicting feelings around sex. There are many reasons why a person might not enjoy it: the two most common are a past history of abuse which leads to unresolved feelings, and the fact that it isn't being done in a way that turns her/him on. A supportive partner (someone who listens without judgment) can make a huge difference, as that feeling of being heard often equates with a feeling of being loved, making it easier for a person to be honest about what is going on, and therefore change it. Many of us are looking for permission to be ourselves. Genuine love is always nonjudgmental and undemanding, and truthfully it is around us all the time. We need to learn how to be in a place where we can embrace that instead of being suspicious and anxious, which creates an atmosphere where the presence of love cannot be felt.

Practice looking people in the eyes, and allowing love to flow from your heart to theirs. You can do this with a stranger you pass in the street, or the checker at the grocery store. We tend to look for love from people we already know, but we can extend unconditional love to anyone at any time, and we can receive it from them. We don't have to have it demonstrated in particular ways; we don't have to be intimate partners. We only have to be willing to offer what we want to receive. Cultivating that ability can create huge shifts in your perception of what is going on around you.

Those three words

Intimacy with another human being is a wonderful thing, and if it includes having great sex, then that is doubly wonderful. As we all know, it is very hard to be intimately involved over time without developing expectations. A relationship that lasts is one where there those expectations unfold easily: in other words, where there is companionship and compatibility and clear communication. How long a relationship lasts, however, is never a measure of its quality. I would measure its quality by how real and honest we can both be, how deeply we can share. In one of my books[7], I wrote the following, which sums it all up: "I want those three little words, *I love you*, to mean, 'I see the wholeness of all that you are in this moment, and I accept you without judgment, honoring your unique infinite beauty. In this moment, my heart is joined with yours and I know that we are not separate beings. I support you absolutely in being fully who you are, even if that means that you will go away and I will never see you again.'"

Presence

Sex is a way of using the body to go beyond the body, reaching to the source of life itself. The human brain can't calculate what is needed to do that. It is a sense of knowing that flows through the body from inside, requiring absolute presence. That's why books about the mechanics of how to have good sex don't work. They can point the way, but this kind of presence can't be taught on an intellectual level. It goes far deeper than the intellect. A good lover can not only facilitate her/his partner's energy flow, but also magnify it by offering exactly what the energy needs: touching another person in exactly the right way, at exactly the right speed, being completely attuned to what

---

[7] Mikaya Heart, *My Sweet Wild Dance*, (Dog Ear Publishing, 2009).

43

is required, without any interference by the intellect. This is what a good healer does too: when someone is sick and goes to a healer (any kind of healer: a Western doctor, a massage therapist, a counselor, a psychic worker) for help, it is that person's job to free up the flow of energy. Most sickness, discomfort, pain, and disease stem from attempting to block energy.

This *being present* is about paying attention and focusing. It is simply committing all of ourselves to bear on the task in hand. When the intellect (the logical mind, the brain, the mental faculties, the thinking process) is in charge and attached to the kind of beliefs I mentioned above, it gets in the way. It takes us a step away from being fully present.

Sex teaches us how to move towards a sensation of pleasure, how to turn away from distractions and focus totally on aligning our bodies so that the energy is able to flow. We can learn how to utilize that ability in many situations. The key is desire, although when it's not sexual, it is often experienced more as a determination, a sense of purpose, a drive, a feeling of rightness. Just as sexual desire makes us throw caution to the winds and give ourselves over completely, so can any kind of desire, enabling an experience of ecstasy that is not associated with the genitals at all. We often call it creativity. Any great creator (and I am talking here about many manifestations of the ability to create: writer, mother, artist, dancer, singer, athlete, builder, etc.) will tell you that it is an orgasmic experience to be able to create freely (unless, as is often true, s/he doesn't want her experience to be associated with sex). Yet creativity is not something we *do*—it's something that flows through us. We lose ourselves in the process, becoming absorbed to the exclusion of all else. While this feeling doesn't usually surge through us in an intense and all-consuming manner like an orgasm, it can still be very powerful. It becomes more of a life habit, a way of being in the world, and less of an isolated event that we seek in order to distract ourselves from the awareness that it is missing from our daily lives.

Sports and art

Apart from sex, the most common arenas for experiencing great surges of energy moving through us are sports, the arts, or intellectual competitions like chess games. Those activities are about bringing one's focus completely into the present, allowing no distractions. I personally recommend the kind of sports that bring you into your body and into relationship with Nature. Kitesurfing (one of my favorite pastimes), for instance, is a dance with water and wind. You cannot fight the forces of wind and water; you must learn to be in tune with their power, and it is a body awareness, since the dozens of tiny movements you need to make every second in order to stay on the board are a body-knowing, far too complex and immediate to be processed by the rational brain. Most people find this kind of pastime profoundly refreshing. When you are out there on the water, everything false falls away and you come back to shore knowing what is true and real. I believe the same thing is true of rock climbing, skiing, wakeboarding, paragliding, motorbike riding, and many other sports. This kind of experience helps people to meet the challenges of daily life with equanimity, enabling them to come into a state of perfect balance in their bodies, freeing up the energy flow that they are.

It's also common to experience this profound feeling of delight when you are with children. They have a natural ability to be present, to be themselves, to be at ease in their bodies, to be exploring the world with excitement and seeing it with eyes that have not already decided what's what. They are willing to be "carried away," and the natural joy that arises from such a free flow is infectious.

The arts have a similar effect. Great artists become absolutely focused in the process of creation. Singing in choirs and dancing in group-formations produce a profound euphoria that is similar to the ecstasy people experience during sex. Team sports such as football produce the same kind of group energy, but those kinds of competitive sports are only a step or two away from political marches where charismatic dictators rouse their followers to violence with provocative speeches. I'd rather see people taking responsibility for themselves on an individual level, learning how to nurture that energy internally and channel it into cooperative ventures.

Sex and feelings

Emotions, or feelings, are the body talking to us, and they are a source of wisdom that never lies, which is why there is a whole chapter in this book about them. Just a few words here, since the

45

need to withhold feelings (a need that all of us experience at one time or another) can prevent us having fulfilling and rewarding sex, because a part of us wants to stop the orgasm that might otherwise open the floodgates. Allowing feelings to flow through us freely is a process that sex can quickly facilitate, and it has enormous repercussions: it is a huge step in the direction of leading a fulfilling and rewarding life. It's not that sex in itself is the answer to life's problems (although research has shown that sex can alleviate a great deal of pain and illness), it's more that it clears away blocks to what is possible. It opens doors to an absolutely different perspective, one that is free from worries and concerns, one where we are simply and fully who we are, and that is all that is necessary. What would happen if we lived from that right-brain[8] perspective on a daily basis? The majority of the things that take up our brain space would simply fall away. We would see with very different eyes and hear with very different ears. We would marvel at the taste and texture of a piece of bread and butter or a grain of rice. We would spend a lot of time appreciating the beauty around us, and our judgments of what is beautiful would change radically, as we interpreted our reality from the present moment instead of from our cultural conditioning. We would operate from a place that was free of judgmental preconceptions—and that is the ultimate definition of freedom.

In the end, however, if sex doesn't turn you on, find something else that does. It's up to you. What inspires you? What calls to you insistently? What makes you sit up and pay attention? What arouses and excites you? Follow that to its source and let it fill you up so you know it in every bone of your body, so that its passion overtakes you to the exclusion of all else. Passion is life force flowing. Give yourself over to it. Let it shake you from the inside out. Feel it to the core of your being.

---

[8] Dr. Jill Bolte-Taylor is a brain researcher who had a serious stroke, which threw her into right brain awareness. She has been able to both talk and write about her experiences, see appendix.

Chapter Five

Less Concrete Reality:
Other Beings and Planets

"There are an infinite number of universes existing side by side
and through which our consciousnesses constantly
pass. In these universes, all possibilities exist." [9]

It may seem strange that a book on how to be in a physical body
refers so much to what is not physical. But, in Truth, our most
familiar state of being is one of pure energy, and it can help us to
understand Truth when we get glimpses of that much greater picture
from which we make the decision to be physical.

Energy is everywhere. Most of us can only see what has
manifested in physical form, or as in the case of wind in the branches
of a tree, we may see its effects. In order to learn how to tap into
some of that energy, it's helpful to have some understanding of the
vastness of the different forms that energy can take even if we can't
(yet) see them. Planet Earth is only in its toddler stages, and as we
grow up, we are beginning to play a part in the cosmos, interacting
with other beings, other worlds, and other universes. In the
meantime, many non-human beings are watching from behind the
scenes and are delighted to be able to help us. Where are they and
how do we contact them? Here are some of my thoughts on this
subject, although I don't pretend to be an expert. (I'm not sure that
any human can be at this point in time.)

---

[9] Paul F. Eno, *Faces at the Window.*

The concept of other dimensions

It's probably most useful first to talk about existence in other dimensions. A being that existed only in the first dimension would simply be a dot. Existing in the second dimension, it would be a line. We all know of the possibilities once it exists in the third dimension. What would the world look like if we were able to see in the fourth dimension? The fifth? Right now, we can't see things that exist in dimensions beyond the third. An amoeba is probably only aware of two dimensions. In relation to what can be visible, perhaps humans are only at the stage of an amoeba.

The inexplicable appearance of light orbs in photographs is a fairly new worldwide phenomenon that is just gaining acceptance, as thousands of people all over the world are getting photos with round lights of varying brightness and hues. I won't go into this in any depth here since other people have written about it[10], but it seems likely that this is the first stage of learning to see fourth dimensional beings.

Why would we think that there are more dimensions? Why wouldn't we? It's another one of those things you can choose to believe. Or not. Some quantum physicists certainly believe in the existence of other dimensions, see appendix.

It is likely that some beings on this planet can pass easily from the third to the fourth dimension. This may explain the occasional sightings and subsequent disappearances of beings that we call Sasquatch or Bigfoot. Hundreds of people have reported seeing them and described them as "melting into the woods." This "melting" is probably exactly what it would look like to watch someone enter another dimension. (Yes, things and beings can just disappear. Don't believe what you were taught.)

The astral realm

Most of us have heard of the astral realm. That's where ghosts hang out, where people go traveling without their bodies, and poltergeists hide. Since we live in a world of duality, everything must have its opposite. The astral realm is the opposite of the physical realm.

---

[10] See Dr. Micheál Ledwith and Joan Ocean in the appendix.

Everything physical has a counterpart in the astral realm. What we would call a ghost is usually the astral counterpart of a physical body. Ideally, the ghost would disappear when the body dies, but sometimes when people die—and particularly when they die in traumatic circumstances and want some resolution to the intensity of emotion surrounding that—the astral part remains, often feeling lost and confused. People who are skilled in the art of psychopomping (from the Greek word ψυχοπομπός or *psuchopompos*, literally meaning the guide of souls) can help it move on. In other words, a psychopomp helps to remove stuck trauma, allowing dead beings to pass to the land of the dead. Wherever that is.

Many psychic healers are shifting things around in the astral realm, sometimes achieving remarkable results. A tricky health situation that doesn't respond well to Western medicine may be addressed very effectively in the astral realm.[11]

Astral traveling and other realms

Many people go traveling in the astral realm without recalling it in their daily lives. It involves leaving the body (usually, but not always asleep) and moving around the world without it. It's an opportunity to visit beings and places that might not otherwise be possible. Most people find the sensation of flying in the astral realm delightful, but they sometimes get scared, seeing their bodies lying still and thinking they won't be able to get back into them. Like everything else, it's a matter of setting the intention that you will return to your body. You can learn to astral travel, but shamanic journeying (see below) is probably easier for most people, and more versatile, since it is about traveling in many realms, not just the astral.

An infinite number of other realms exist. Planets can be understood as planes of consciousness. They may exist in other dimensions, in parallel realities, or in other realms. I cannot explain what any of those words and phrases actually refer to, although anyone who has studied quantum physics in depth may have some idea. I am using the word *realm* simply because it seems to fit. I don't know what makes a realm a realm or not. I do know that all of these

[11] Mikaya Heart, *With the Sun in My Eyes*: this book is about a woman who does wonderful healing work in the astral realm.

can occur within the illusion of physicality—which, remember, is a delightful and wonderful thing. I am not talking about the vastness of All-that-we-are. That exists outside physicality. It is not part of the illusion. It creates the illusion, infusing life into it.

Many other beings occupy these various realms, and they may share some of the same space with us, perhaps in different dimensions. They may at times affect us, although usually in ways that we are not directly aware of, since they are invisible to us. You don't have to believe in them, and you don't have to know anything about the specifics of them. You probably never have to have anything to do with any of them, although you may want to, simply because they are interesting and can occasionally be a source of great assistance.

Spirits

The word spirit is often used to refer to any non-physical life-form, although people, animals, trees, rocks, plants, rivers, oceans, hills, valleys, lakes—all places of Nature—have spirits that represent their life-force. Plant spirits are often called *devas*. My grandmother, who was an incredible gardener, could see the beings associated with specific plants, and she identified them as fairies. I believe that her skill as a gardener was a consequence of her ability to relate to each plant as an individual sentient being. She could hear each plant telling her its specific needs, and they did well because they enjoyed being acknowledged as individuals.

This kind of communication comes from the heart, rather than being spoken with the voice or heard with the ears. Perhaps you feel peaceful whenever you lean up against a particular tree. Perhaps you feel called to put your hand on a rock wall. Perhaps you feel that the sound of a river flowing is singing to you. Perhaps a deer is always watching when you walk by a particular spot. Honor these things. Everything in Nature wants to be admired, just as we all do. Take a moment to appreciate these expressions of life flowing. If you're going sailing and the wind is just right, offer thanks for a gentle ride. If you were going to go sailing and the ocean was too wild, offer thanks that she did not swallow you up. Offer thanks to all things in

Nature, and don't assume that you have the right to cut down trees or dig up the earth without considering the spirits that may be displaced or disturbed.

When we make friends with the Nature spirits around us, they can be delightful and very helpful allies. Many humans already make friends with them without even realizing what they are doing. Have you ever picked up a beautiful rock and brought it home? You think you found the stone, but in Truth it's more likely that it found you. Although you can ignore its request to be picked up, these kinds of interactions are exchanges of love, and will make you feel good. We think we are the ones in charge, the ones making the decisions, and we are frequently wrong. Acknowledging how much we are unaware of is a step in embracing the humility that is an essential aspect of being fully alive.

The power of Nature

Spending time alone in natural surroundings, away from the presence of humans and artificial sounds, lights, and materials is an experience I recommend strongly. I don't just mean going for walks. That's great, but you can learn a great deal by spending long periods of time sitting or sleeping in natural surroundings, with no walls between you and the magnificent outdoors. I recommend that you don't take any books, radio, movies, recorded music, or anything that will distract you from being present. Bring some writing material so you can record what you experience, but limit that to a short time every day. By all means bring a musical instrument and your own voice so you can sing and dance as a gift to your surroundings.

Over time, this will enable you to access some deep wisdom. It's partly the presence of spirits and the unconditional love that you will begin to feel emanating from the trees, rocks, plants, animals and the Earth itself. Most of us can feel that kind of love from pets or other animals that we are familiar with. The problem there is the same as it is with people: we focus on whom or what is facilitating the experience, without realizing that it is a gateway. Love is constantly emanating all around us. When we are alone in natural surroundings, we can allow ourselves to feel it more easily. Humans tend to be conditional with their loving, and constantly judgmental about the person to whom they are giving it. Things of Nature are not conditional about their love.

The longer you spend doing this, the more you will begin to get in touch with something else. I'm not even sure how to describe it: perhaps that phrase, the vastness of being, is appropriate here. It is some other aliveness that is willing to relate to us when we are able to be fully present. I have been left almost breathless with the power of this sensation at times. It is more than the spirits, or devas, that take form as trees and plants—I sense them too, and this is something else.

A friend once asked me what I do when I am alone in Nature. I said, "I dream." I might also say, "I listen." I practice just being.

One further point here: I have spoken with a number of socially conscientious people who believe that beings of Nature are angry with humans, or at least, not willing to extend love to us, because they believe that we are destroying the planet. Although some humans are acting disrespectfully out of greed and fear, it is manifestly untrue that we are all destroying it, and it's somewhat arrogant to think that we could, since the forces that are taking care of this planet are much more powerful than we are. We are an integral part of life on this Earth, and as such, we are loved, because all life is loved. The more alive we are (and as I have said earlier, some people are trying not to be fully alive), the more we will experience that love.

I have a friend who felt the presence of an aboriginal elder when she visited the cave where that person had been buried. She said the elder was really angry and considered all white people stupid. While it is understandable to think that stupidity is a common human attribute, my friend is not a stupid person, and if you are reading this book you probably aren't either. Occasionally you may get in touch with beings that are angry with the human race. You need to ask yourself, are you acting with as much respect as you are able? If so, it doesn't benefit you to take on negative judgments made by an angry person. Some spiritual practices encourage people to get in touch with their ancestors and make a regular practice of appeasing them. I question whether this is appropriate. Occasionally dead people, such as the aboriginal elder mentioned above, are stuck in the astral realm and holding onto emotions that are associated with the physical realm. Once such a being has moved beyond the astral realm, those emotions dissipate, and the being may be able to be present for you in a nonjudgmental and supportive way. I have found this is true of my now-dead father, who has become a very beneficial presence that is with me daily, in spite of the fact that we had an acrimonious relationship while he was alive.

Become familiar with the forces of Nature. Stand on a cliff top and let the wind blow your hair back from your face. Walk in a river and feel the current pulling at your legs. Let an ocean wave knock you over. Weep at the beauty of a sunset, at the endless variation of the cloudscapes. Watch a rainstorm gather and allow the deluge to soak you through. Lie still in the timeless silence of night-time in the deep forest. Listen to the bird songs and other sounds. Go snorkeling and look fish in the eye, as they look at you. Pick a leaf off a bush, feel its texture in your fingers, put it in your mouth and taste it. Walk barefoot. Lean your forehead against the trunk of a tree and allow yourself to hear its song. These are truly spiritual practices.

Developing awareness of non-human beings

Nature spirits are associated with some physical form such as a tree or a rock. We are constantly surrounded by spirits, or beings, that have no physical form visible to us. Those in the astral realm may be left over from a time when they were physical, but there are many other realms in which spirits exist. The awareness of them comes through more strongly in certain places, such as the Middle East, where many well-known prophets felt the sensation of presence and interpreted it as the voice of God. Some of the unseen spirits around us are simply seeking attention in the same way that some physical beings do, and their intentions are not for the highest good. How can you be sure that you are not interacting with a being that does not wish you well? It's all about setting your own intention clearly. Do you only wish to interact with others who are concerned about the highest good of all? State that as your intention. Know it fully. Other beings will recognize you for who you are, and make their choices accordingly. Beings of integrity will not reveal themselves to someone who is not coming from a place of integrity. Beings with intentions that you would experience as undesirable will not be able to reach you if your intention is pure.

You don't have to consider yourself psychic to feel the presence of another being, dead or alive, human or otherwise, or to send and receive messages from them. We tend to think it's very unusual to communicate telepathically—without spoken or written words, sometimes over long distances—but that is mainly because we have learned not to give any credit to the messages that come to us by methods other than physical.

There is an important aspect to the concept of telepathy: you cannot lie when you are communicating without words. There can be no pretense, no pleasantly meaningless niceties. The truth of what you are thinking will be constantly transparent. Since human culture has for many centuries depended on people being able to deceive each other, the development of the ability to read thoughts will involve radical changes in our society—changes very pleasing to some of us, and terrifying to others.

Messages and information are being offered to us all the time, from many sources. The more we start paying attention to them, the more they will occur. These messages are not necessarily profound; they may just be a greeting or an amusing remark. Many non-humans like to have fun and don't value gravity. Perhaps an odd thought pops up in your brain for no apparent reason. It might be a thought about someone you know or have known. Maybe you dismiss it because you are busy. Go back to it when you have time, and allow it to develop into a conversation. Play with it; allow your imagination free rein. If you don't know what to say, you can simply project love. You may find yourself rolling your eyes at the path the conversation takes in your head, so drop it, and let it be. Perhaps it will come back again and perhaps not, but you may be surprised at how often a friend will call you soon after you have been thinking about him or her. Remember that just because a dead person cannot call or text does not mean she or he has not been thinking about you.

Some people are aware of a physical sensation of presence. Perhaps you get a prickly feeling when something dangerous is nearby, or you find yourself wanting to take another route rather than the one you usually take to work. Perhaps you dream intensely about something or someone. Perhaps you find extraordinary coincidences occurring in your vicinity. Honor all of these for what they are—messages and assistance from other realms. Often the communication is in the form of a feeling rather than words, which are limited. In the case of remarkable synchronicity or coincidences, maybe the Universe is saying to you, "Look what can be done!" You are being informed that you can use this unlimited source of power consciously, by setting a clear intention.

One word of warning here: we were born into this physical realm because this is where we want to focus. Don't fall into the trap of abandoning your body and spending most of your time in other realities beyond this world, because that is antithetical to the art of being fully alive in human form. Occasional journeying in other realms is great, and you can access a great deal of assistance and wisdom that way, but make sure you come back home to your physical body and apply what you have been offered to what is going on here.

Psychics

In order to function in our physical world we need to be able to filter out the majority of what is going on around us, and most of us learn to do that as we grow up. It's part of what occurs as we learn to walk: we identify a table as a table, seeing its edges and feeling it as solid. We figure out the physical boundaries of our own bodies, and most of us cease to see energy. Some, however, do not. We generally call such people psychics, and there has always been a certain cultural fascination with them, although they are often dismissed as crazy by those who are attached to the idea that the physical world is all there is. New Agers might say that it must be wonderful to be psychic—but think about it for a minute. If you could see that someone has cancer or is about to have an accident of some kind, what are you going to do? The person might not want to hear what you have to say, and the only effect of your warnings might be to throw her/him into turmoil. Psychics constantly have to deal with these kinds of dilemmas even when the people who come to them think they want to hear what is being said. It's not an easy way to live your life, and a high proportion of drug and alcohol addicts are people who are trying to drown out such perceptions.

So being psychic can be a lonely path. Sometimes people only make friends with you because they think you have access to a kind of wisdom that they also want to be able to access. Many psychics end up invested in an image of being the one who knows everything—and since no one, even the most accomplished psychic in the world, can really tell someone else what to do, which is not a desirable state. All of us can tap into a source of personal inner wisdom, which will inform us of everything we need to know—and that is far more valuable and truthful than any external source.

Shamanic journeying

Shamanic journeying[12] is a useful skill, similar to lucid dreaming, and easier for most people to practice. Although it's called journeying, it may not involve a sensation of movement. It's a way of tapping into universal wisdom. Originally, shamans of indigenous tribes would use the sound of the drum or the rattle to go on this kind of journey to bring back parts of a person's soul that had split off as a result of some trauma (Western psychologists might refer to this as a split personality). I have led journeys for many different people and in my experience almost anyone can travel in this way. You can put it all down to your imagination. It really doesn't matter. It is a way of accessing the vastness of being, and people often come back from a shamanic journey with useful information that they could not access in any other way—except perhaps from sleeping dreams or visions.

It may be that a journeyer returns without any specific memory but with a strong feeling of being refreshed and rejuvenated. The rational brain doesn't always allow us to bring the memories to the surface of our consciousness. If you think you are blocking memories that you want to retrieve, you can work with setting the intention to recall them, and requesting all those rational voices that think this is rubbish to give you space. You may have to be both firm and reassuring since the logical side of you often thinks it has to be on guard and in charge. On the other hand, not being able to bring a memory into your everyday concrete reality doesn't detract from the value of journeying. Much of what is occurring around us and

---

[12] A recording of my invocation and shamanic journey is available on my website, mikayaheart.org.

affecting us enormously is doing so outside our rational awareness. Huge internal shifts can happen without any conscious involvement of the mind. They may even require that!

Shamanic journeying enables a personal experience that can be tremendously empowering. It's all well and good that you are reading this book, but reading what someone else says is a far cry from experiencing it yourself. Journeying is a direct way of accessing your own knowing.

Shamanism and shamanic thinking

Shamanic ways of thinking about reality are profound. Throughout history, there have been many stories of shamans such as the witches of Europe and the medicine people of Native American tribes. *The Teachings of Don Juan: A Yaqui Way Of Knowledge*, by Carlos Castaneda, published in 1968, was the first book on shamanism to be widely read in the West. Don Juan was a member of the Toltec lineage, sorcerers (or shamans) from Southern Mexico. I have heard that there are several different lineages from that area focusing on different paths and teachings. Not being born or trained into such traditions, I cannot verify the truth of anything about the Toltecs, but I find much of what has been written about them both fascinating and educational.

Modern shamans in the West do healing work such as soul retrievals and energy clearing. Many alternative healers are utilizing what might be called shamanic work of various kinds, sometimes without being aware of what they are doing on a conscious level. A reminder here on the concept of consciousness: we are all very active on a deep subconscious level, and we often choose not to bring that to surface consciousness because it would be overwhelming for our physical form. We can still act with complete integrity (or not) without having a rational-brain awareness of what we've been doing. Our language is not adequate to explain these concepts, since in Truth, we are always one hundred percent aware, or conscious. But, to refer to my previous metaphor, your thumb doesn't have to know what your liver is doing.

A shaman is able to work with energy in other realms so that things are altered in this physical realm that we all know. Really, that is all that we are doing when we manifest something. The difference is that a shaman has developed his or her abilities to a fine degree, and can consciously move in other realms, shaping energy and shifting it around, and relating to other beings. The rest of us, even when we journey in other realms, are rarely quite so deliberate, although probably anyone can learn to be so. Shamanic play is powerful and effective. It is about moving beyond standard ideas of time and place, frequently working in apparently miraculous ways.

Time and place

Time is an artificial (and very useful) construct, and we can practice making it fit our plans, rather than forcing our plans to fit into it. Recall the taste of something delicious; let's say a strawberry. Perhaps when you last ate a strawberry, you got distracted and forgot to be really with it as you crunched it up in your mouth. You can go back to that time and savor the taste of the juices now. Or you know you are going to eat a strawberry later today, and you imagine right now exactly how it will taste, exactly what its texture is. At first it's not as good as the real thing, but with practice you can catch the fullness of it.

We only know that time exists because of place, which is space, where physical reality manifests. All physical things change over time, and it is only those changes that enable us to mark the passage of time. If everything always remained the same, we would never have any idea what time it is. Shamans understand how illusory these constructs of time and place really are, and work outside them. A person who thinks shamanically is not tied to a limited perception of reality. This makes them more powerful than the average person, because they see more potential in life. They see much more of life.

Guides

I started this chapter saying that there are many other beings around who want to help us. While that is certainly true, everything we need to know flows from inside. Our inner wisdom is infinite, and will never lie to us. That said, we are humans, and we often find it both delightful and useful to relate to sources that are apparently outside of us.

58

Some people believe that they have a particular guide or guides who are with them all their lives. Sometimes they are identified as beings of light, or angels, which *are* beings of light. They may be in the form of power animals. Some people believe they have specific power animals that are always with them; I've found they change from time to time, coming to me when I need the particular characteristics that animal embodies. Several books have been written on the qualities represented by specific species of animals. However, these external references are like interpreting dreams or cards; in the end, we are all different and what an animal, a dream, or a card means to you may not be what the book says. I'd advise you to believe yourself first.

No matter how you perceive it, you may be sure that there is plenty of assistance available for you in every situation. So make a practice of remembering that you are not alone and asking for help whenever you need it. Just say in your mind as though you are addressing someone else: "I need help with this, please," or any variation of that. This asking and being willing to receive help is important, because your guides (or helpers, or whatever you want to call them) cannot help you until they are requested to do so. It's one of those universal laws. Since they want to help (that's what they are hanging around for), they will be happy when you do ask. Whenever you find yourself wondering how you are going to be able to manage this, or feeling annoyed because you forgot the instructions on how to get where you are going, or alarmed because you realize you are probably going to be late, or afraid because it's dark and you can't see what is around you, or anxious because you've lost that important piece of paper—just stop and ask for help. Any time, for any reason, just ask for help. Often when you do so, things suddenly resolve themselves easily and smoothly.

You can specifically access your guides through a shamanic journey or a guided visualization, or ask them to come to you in a dream. They may appear as archetypes or childhood heroes or heroines. Don't limit yourself. My most powerful guide is a loving presence, so powerful that the word guide doesn't do it justice. It is a sense of guidance, an awareness that I am taken care of on a very deep level. It would be limiting for me to personify this presence— it's not an individual, and even if it might at times appear to me to be a particular being, it's not confined to that being.

Our guides are leading their own lives, as we are leading ours. As I said earlier, we are all doing many different things in many different places all at once. You may be operating as a guide for others, without ever being consciously aware of this.

No matter how many guides we have, we still need to make our own choices and take responsibility for our own lives. The message from our guides might be that we are taking life too seriously, which can cause us to be stuck in agonizing indecision because we are afraid of making a mistake. Sometimes it doesn't even matter what the decision is as long as it gets us moving. Changing your mind is always an option, and there is no such thing as wasted time.

Other ways of finding guidance

Sometimes guidance comes through in specific ways at specific moments. Perhaps a raven will come and sit on a fence talking to you; perhaps a book falls off a shelf at your feet, open at a particular page; perhaps you lose your way and find yourself somewhere that you would never otherwise have gone. Pay attention to these happenings. They are not accidents.

Praying is simply a way of talking to yourself, although you may think of it as addressing a specific deity, entity or the Universe itself—and that's a fine way to see it. When you are asking for guidance, you can concentrate energy deliberately by meditating, or by calling in directions, which many indigenous people do, or by setting a circle, which is a Wiccan tradition. In these ways, you invoke a sense of the sacred, which adds to the energy of setting an intention. There are no rules about the way you do any of these, unless you decide that you want to do them according to a particular pre-set method.

We are being guided as a planet. One example of this is the crop circles that have been appearing all over the world, most commonly in England. These circles are extraordinary. I will not go into the topic in detail here since others have written about them, see appendix. Some crop circles are man-made and some are certainly not. The obvious question is: What are they for? Do they contain some kind of encoded message that we need to unravel? Perhaps so, but I think the answer may be simpler. A friend of mine said cynically, "Well, whatever the message is, we're obviously not getting it!"

"Yes, we are," I replied. "Anyone who looks at those crop circles and says, 'Wow!' is getting the message."

If non-human beings want to communicate with us, why don't they appear in front of us and talk? What they are communicating could not be said in words. And no one who is sending a message of magnitude is going to want to deal with the global arguments and political machinations that would result from the appearance of a bunch of visitors from another planet.

Imagination, a powerful tool

Your imagination is a useful tool and fun to play with. You can practice imagining all kinds of fun things, and as always, you can control where your imagination goes—it is only thinking. If it runs away with you, and you don't like where it's going, then deliberately focus on something that pleases you.

People often believe that shamanic journeying stems from their imaginations. That's fine. Wherever those journeys arise from, they can be enjoyable, informative, and deeply relaxing. You can use your imagination to create sacred spaces and call in energy to achieve whatever you want. Set an intention, create a rite of passage, strengthen a prayer, or commit to something. That's what a wedding is, and all the palaver associated with it makes the commitment more binding simply because it makes it a very memorable occasion. You can use all kinds of props to help you to build the energy, for instance, dress up, draw a circle in the dirt or on the floor, sing songs, light candles, build a fire, call in the elements, address the directions, speak directly with spirits or archetypes or other human beings who are not physically present. Choose your timing to correspond with the seasons, the equinoxes, the solstices, or your own birthday. Call upon the Universe, ask for help, and state your request aloud.

Always say thank you afterwards. Gratitude is important. If you express gratitude, you will find more and more things to be grateful for. Above all, appreciate yourself and all the opportunities available to you. You are a priceless being. So is everyone else. Treat yourself that way and treat everyone else that way.

Your rational mind may often ridicule the above activities. One way to keep it happy is to do some kind of official study of these things. Teachers and groups doing this kind of work are springing up all over the world. Choose one and immerse yourself in it. Meeting others who are practicing these things will help you to accept them as "real," and then you can get to the point of developing your own ideas, and finding what works specifically for you. When I was first learning, I did a number of ceremonial fire walks. We really walked on fire. I could see and feel how our initial ritual built the energy, and it was different from anything I had deliberately done before. My rational mind argued that the coals were not hot enough to burn us, but I couldn't know that for sure and some serious questioning was begun.

Yes and no

I have said that you must learn not to push away what you don't want, but that doesn't mean you have to put up with anything and everything. We need to learn to maintain our own personal energetic space so that other energies cannot easily push us off balance. Being able to say no to what you don't want is just as important as saying yes to what you do want. Develop an awareness of what is your own personal space, and what or whom you are choosing to allow in that space. You can firmly tell another being or a thought or any other energy that it is not welcome. You can also invite other beings in—although they may not accept your invitation, just as you might choose not to pick up that stone that is calling you.

If you have had other beings or other energies in your space for a long time—and it is fairly common for people or beings who have been very intimate to get into each other's space—it may not be so easy to get them out, because it is an old familiar habit to have them there. But it's like changing any habit: it's a matter of observation, decision, focus, and commitment. See Chapter Eight.

Chapter Six

Ego and Self

"Don't believe me, don't believe yourself,
and don't believe anybody else." [13]

We've all had our individual stories, an image that we are projecting, and a self that we want to be or think we ought to be. Those things are transitory and change-able. Problems arise when we get stuck in them, when we are attached to maintaining them. Most of us have a particular idea about what is good and bad, what is difficult in life, and why it is that way, and what happened in the past to make it so, and what needs to happen in the future. These stories may have some truth to them and we may have good reasons to believe them, but it really doesn't matter. What matters is now, this moment now, and what we decide to be in this moment. Usually our stories about the past hold us in a rigid pattern that is very limiting, especially if we often repeat them to others, which reinforces them. If you want to make changes in your life, practice *not* telling your standard stories, even when they seem unrelated to the changes you want to make.

We *can* let go of all the past in one split second of clear, un-contradicted decision, moving immediately into a completely new way of being in the world, transforming our belief systems instantaneously. It often takes hitting rock bottom to do that. Eckhart Tolle, Jan Frazier, and Byron Katie[14] were three regular Westerners who hit rock bottom, and that is what provided the motivation they needed to achieve what might be called a state of

---

[13] Don Miguel Ruiz, *The Four Agreements: A Practical Guide to Personal Freedom.*

[14] All of these people are now teachers, see appendix.

enlightenment. It happened overnight and the change was so radical that they can no longer be called regular Westerners. It is probably possible for anyone to make radical and sudden changes of this kind, but it can be done more gradually, and that may be easier on our physical, mental, and emotional bodies, as well as our friends.

Being attached to stories and knowing nothing

Humans have explanations for everything. They vary from how the Earth came to be and concepts of evolution, to why President Obama was elected, to the family genes that have made you a likely candidate for breast cancer, to how and why your mother neglected you when you were little. Having explanations satisfies the rational brain, that monkey mind that has such a tendency to be scornful and suspicious. Whether or not they are true really doesn't matter. The satisfaction that we feel from maintaining them at all costs and proving them to be true, often in order to substantiate that we are right and good, is a shallow kind of egotistical satisfaction that maintains a shallow and egotistical way of being in the world. I strongly suggest practicing the art of not-knowing, or as Angeles Arrien put it, "being in the land of gray clouds."[15] To think that we even *can* know is part of our wonderful illusion. If you are looking for a teacher, my advice is to ask her or him, "What do you know?" If the answer is, "I know nothing!" you may have found someone worth studying with.

How can it be that a good teacher knows nothing? Perhaps *you* will think that she does know something, but the fact that *she* knows she really knows nothing is a good start. There is no way to explain the experience of knowing that you know nothing. It's the same with knowing that "I am that." Once you have that experience, you understand it. Until then, it's Greek. If you keep on trying to grasp it with the rational brain, you will remain in a place where you cannot get it at all. Just accept that you don't understand it.

You can't pretend these things. When you actually experience that you are *that*, and you know nothing, you will feel relief. You're no longer trying to get something that cannot be got.

---

[15] Angeles Arrien, *The Four-Fold Way: Walking the Paths of the Warrior, Teacher, Healer and Visionary*. (HarperCollins, 1993).

Your inner wisdom

The odd thing about teaching is that no teacher can teach a student something the student doesn't already know. In the same way, you cannot ask a question to which you don't already know the answer. The teacher's job is simply to help you discover your own answer, your own knowing, and your own inner wisdom. You might think of it as getting rid of all the layers under which the answer is hiding. Don Miguel Ruiz and Byron Katie are both writers and teachers who can help you in that process, see appendix. The bottom line is always questioning the surface stories, the standard explanations, other people, and yourself. Your standard beliefs (and other people's beliefs, or at least the ones that you are considering at any given time) are layers that cover the Truth, that are hiding your answers. That occurs on every level, cultural as well as personal.

Your own knowing is the only knowing that is of any real use to you. And you don't have to have a teacher to get in touch with it, although few of us really manage to do so without a little external help, even when that external help is pushing us to understand what I said at the beginning of the last paragraph.

Becoming a witness

Start watching yourself and others when telling stories. What stories are you attached to? What stories bring you a sense of relief? How deep does that relief go? How long does it last? Do you get angry when you feel the relief of those stories slipping out of your grasp? Can you imagine what an immense relief it would be to know something—or rather nothing at all—that would take away all the grasping once and for all?

The ability to look at oneself, to indulge in ongoing, in-depth self-examination without condemnatory self-judgment, is an essential tool for people who want to reach beyond duality. When you've been doing that for a while, you can begin to see what is really motivating you. This is a situation where the rational brain is essential. Ask yourself questions until you get to the root of what you need to do to improve the quality of your life. Let's assume that you've discovered you live with a constant undercurrent of anxiety (which is extremely common). Here's how you might discover that: ask yourself, do you want that ice cream because the taste is delightful? Or, are you cleaning the sink for the third time today because it needs it? Are you craving ice cream or cleaning the sink because you are feeling anxious and it will comfort you? There is nothing wrong with this, but I'd recommend you address what is making you feel anxious. Do you feel anxious most of the time? What is it you are afraid of? That you can't live up to cultural expectations? That people won't like you? That you will lose your job? That you aren't a good person? That your partner will leave you? That you won't be able to pay the rent? That you will die? Do you believe that the world is a dangerous place and you need to be constantly on guard? Imagine a life where you didn't feel anxious. What would it look like? What do you need to change to be living that life?

I am not saying that it is easy to address this undercurrent of anxiety that so many of us live with. It may take time and serious commitment. I *am* saying it's essential you don't allow it to be a motivating force in your life.

Thinking, or worrying, that you are not a good person is very common. Judgments of 'good' and 'bad' are always suspect because they involve comparing ourselves to others, or trying to measure up to a standard set externally by someone else or by the culture. You may know yourself well enough to be aware of your inner motivations, so you know when your motivation for a good deed is self-aggrandizement, and you may get down on yourself about it, not realizing that this is a common human habit. Everyone else is doing it too, and no one else is talking about it Are you doing your best? Are your intentions genuinely kind? Then forgive yourself. We weren't meant to be born without what we consider faults, and having faults doesn't make you any different from anyone else. You're human. How would it feel to know that you are perceived as a delightful being by many entities that don't relate to concepts of good and bad? I can assure you that there are many beings (some human, some not) that love you unconditionally, just the way you are right now. Decide that you want to get in touch with them.

Believing that life is too difficult and you can't do it alone is another one. How about if you knew that you didn't have to do it alone and there was an infinite source of assistance always available to you? You can decide to get in touch with that source.

Being afraid of dying is another common fear, and not a useful fear to live with. What would make you unafraid of dying? Knowing that you live forever, perhaps? Then allow yourself to wonder if you could live forever. That wondering, if you allow it, will take you to the most important question of all, the question that underlies all other questions, perhaps the only question that requires answering: who is that *you*?

You don't have to believe that life is forever, that we are all magnificent beings, and that there are hundreds of beings cheering for us, in order to study the art of being human. If you did already believe those things, you would already be well on your way to mastery. You just have to think that there is some possibility, however faint, that life would be better if you go ahead and work on the assumption that some of my beliefs are true. Then you decide to give it a go.

Being who you are and letting go of judgment

Nothing that you do, nothing that you achieve, no physical possession, no belief system, and no other person can be as important as who you are. Everything you create, which is you and everything around you, is a reflection of who you are. That's why you chose to be born. Be who you are, and be proud of who you are, knowing that everyone else is also unique and magnificent—and different. Honor yourself and honor everyone else. You are no better or worse than anyone else, and there is no one any better or worse than you.

On the other hand, don't get attached to who you are at any particular moment. Attachment to looking or behaving a particular way, or to projecting an image and being seen as a particular kind of person, will limit you. Let your self change on a daily basis, and be excited by that. Allow this manifestation, what you are in any given moment, to change and develop on every level. The Truth is that everything is changing all the time. Instead of resisting that change and trying to adhere to a static view of yourself and the world, allow yourself to be in the natural flow.

Practice letting go of judgment about how things ought to be. Accept everything exactly as it is right now, without any idea of changing it. Observe yourself and the life going on around you without the eyes of judgment that most human beings have adopted. See that all is well, that in this moment *nothing needs to be changed*. The paradox is that accepting the fullness of this moment exactly as it is, without desiring to change it, enables you to move on from it if you wish. Feeling critical and negative about a situation traps you in it. Accept it completely and know whether or not you wish to stay in it.

I am not telling you to put up endlessly with something that is unpleasant. The ability to do that is not useful. I am telling you to learn to perceive that things that are unpleasant don't need to be destroyed. They are not wrong or bad, and it is not your job to fix them. You only need to take responsibility for your own life. That means that you need to discern clearly what feels good to you, and consistently place yourself there. I am not necessarily referring to physical placement, though that is frequently relevant.

Chapter Seven

Feelings and Beliefs

"Life is simple. Everything happens for you, not to you." [16]

Feelings, or emotions, affect us all, and are rarely understood in this society because the rational brain has been so deeply revered, and feelings often appear quite *irrational*. Any student of the art of being human wants to study feelings since they are always about allowing energy to flow. Here is a quick primer:

1. Feelings are not facts, but they often affect us much more than facts.

2. Feelings may carry tremendous energy, which makes them very powerful.

3. Trying to rationalize someone out of a feeling ("There's no reason to be so angry about it!") is not likely to make someone feel better, although it may enable him or her to see that the original basis for the feeling does not stem from the present situation.

4. Feelings always want to be felt and they can pass quickly when you allow yourself to express them fully.

5. Feelings that we do not allow ourselves to feel in the moment they arise hang around, maybe forever, waiting for an opportunity to be expressed. These old stuck feelings sap our energy and effectively prevent us from being clear channels of energy.

---

[16] Byron Katie, *Loving What Is*. (Harmony, 2002).

6. If you do clear out old feelings, you will find the new feelings that come up are always related to the present situation and they are hugely informative. Every feeling has something to tell you.

You can see that it is a good idea to pay attention to feelings. If they are triggered in a way that seems out of proportion to the present moment, then you have been storing them from the past. Addressing the past and letting them move on is well worth the effort. Sitting on feelings because they are judged inappropriate (by you or anyone else) is a major source of stress and tension in modern society.

Never try to rationalize a feeling away. You feel what you feel. There is always a reason for feelings, always something that makes them come up, but you don't necessarily have to know what that reason is. Simply know they are always valid (even if they are from the past), without requiring any rational explanation. They never lie. They are specific to you. The person standing next to you may have quite different feelings from you. That's fine.

It is part of the skill of being human to let feelings pass through you without blaming others. Blaming others or yourself is never a useful way of dealing with life. On the other hand, a feeling may be telling you to get away from a particular situation. Once again, you don't need to justify that. Simply do what your feelings are telling you.

Letting old feelings pass

If you never make any big changes in your life, you may be able to keep old feelings under control for many years without ever being consciously aware that you are doing that. When you choose something different in your life, old stuck feelings from the past often come up: fear, sadness, pain, and lack of self-worth, for instance. You may need to give yourself plenty of space to feel those difficult feelings, *with the intention of letting them pass*. You must allow yourself to feel them fully, without trying to restrain them. If it is a violent feeling, you may have to restrain its physical expression—that is different from restraining the feeling itself. You want to be able to embrace the feeling completely, without any effort to avoid it.

70

You can't banish emotions completely until they have moved through you, but you can command them to move through you speedily and then depart. You can also command them to wait. If you are in the middle of a negotiation with someone, for instance, and you are suddenly aware of intense anger, you don't want that anger to move through you right then. Tell it to wait till you are ready. Then, when you are ready, invite its presence, stating that you are now letting it move through you so that it can pass on. Here is the important part: you must ground yourself in the here and now as the emotion arises. Think of yourself in the center of the crosshairs of this moment, like making an X on a piece of paper. Then breathe and allow. You may need to make sounds, you may experience intense swirling, you may have some vivid images, it may take several minutes or longer, and then it is gone. Sounds too easy? It does require courage, because most of us are afraid of being overpowered by an intense emotion. It helps to maintain a conscious awareness that you are choosing this. It's not a wave that suddenly comes and overwhelms you. You are in charge and you are willing to be immersed in it for a brief time period *so that it will pass.*

All emotions have gifts, so be receptive to that. It could be a feeling of love, a new understanding and awareness, or a sense of relief.

Healers have developed a number of simple ways of helping stuck feelings to move on: for instance, the Emotional Freedom Technique, which involves tapping on the meridians. Some of these methods are quick and efficient, but you may want to find a counselor to help you make the shift. One of the problems you may come up against is that feelings don't respond to talk therapy, since they do not arise in the rational brain, where talk therapy is based. There are many ways of working with the body and with visualizations to change old stuck stuff. Find out what works for you. You might decide to go with a life coach as a source of assistance, because a coach is more likely to be guided from a heart-space and is less stuck in mental ways of working than traditional therapists. In the end, it doesn't matter a great deal what a person's qualifications are; it matters how they vibrate with you.

Perhaps you are simply addicted to an old habit of feeling a particular way, so that the feeling keeps recurring. You can change any ingrained habit. It takes commitment.

Singing, toning, or making any sound, is an excellent method of self-expression that may help feelings move. It is also a good idea to express feelings through body movement since they are often held in the body. Move your body regularly and feel how it speaks to you as you move it. Dancing is a wonderful skill to learn since it is not only a way of expressing yourself, it also teaches you how to hear and feel rhythms.

Feelings give rise to thoughts, and thoughts to feelings. They are part of the endless cycle of life. I'm going to talk now about thoughts since it is easier to address and change thoughts before they manifest as feelings.

Changing the way you think

A belief is simply a thought that is so habitual you don't notice you're thinking it. You can change your thoughts or beliefs with some concentrated focus. Your present beliefs don't need to rule what you do, because you can always change them. You don't have to trust that what I am suggesting will work before you start. If you are committed to giving it a go, you will find yourself trusting it at some point in the process (or perhaps you will give up).

Our minds' interpretations of our current belief systems are not always up to date. For instance, we may have a secret interest in something that most of the people we know find ridiculous. We keep that interest a secret from ourselves because we don't want to appear ridiculous, and we actually persuade ourselves we do not believe this thing. One day we meet someone who does believe it. Out of habit, we may assert that we do not believe it, but the sense of intrigue has been revived. It's always wonderful to allow the smidgeon of belief that has been waiting inside to voice itself, although it sometimes takes time and courage. As an example, I met someone who heard that I lead shamanic journeys. He asked what that means and I gave a brief explanation. Looking slightly pained, he said, "You don't really believe in that stuff, do you?"

"Yes," I replied with a smile, and changed the subject to something less charged. Later that day, he came up to me and said, "You know, I'd like to try one of these shamanic journeys."

It wasn't so much that he believed shamanic journeys are rubbish, as he believed he *ought* to think they are rubbish. There is a big difference.

Many beliefs are based very deeply in our subconscious so that we are unaware of them until we come up against them. Our feelings can make us aware of them. For instance, if you have a stab of fear when someone suggests doing a shamanic journey, it may be that you believe it is a dangerous thing to do. Or perhaps you are afraid you won't be able to do it. Then you need to look at whether you want to maintain those beliefs. If you want to change them, you may have to do something to alter your attitude. Often it is simply a matter of investigating what is really involved in a shamanic journey, or whatever is frightening you. Or, you may investigate it and find you really don't want to do it.

Fear, anger, grief, and pain

Sometimes being in the presence of a particular person will inspire a sensation of fear or dislike. It may be that person's energy is simply antithetical to us—vibrating at a very different frequency—or that the person reminds us of someone else, or that there is some residue from another lifetime when you knew this person, or that you are picking up the other person's feelings. If the feeling continues beyond the first meeting, I'd recommend paying attention and staying away from that person. Forcing ourselves to do anything that feels wrong is unwise, no matter how irrational it may seem.

Fear and its attendant sensations, such as anxiety, trepidation, or terror, are rarely useful except when they tell us that our bodies are in danger. It's useful to experience fear when a car is about to hit us, and we need to get out of the way fast (or, as in the paragraph above when we need to get away from a person). Anger and its attendant sensations, such as annoyance, irritation, or fury, are useful when they are informing us that something needs to change, and we then take an appropriate course of action to create the change. Experiencing fear or anger on an ongoing daily basis is a sure indication that we are not paying attention to the messages we are being offered by All-that-we-are. Perhaps it's such an old habit that we are barely aware of the possibility of being in some other state. Perhaps it makes us feel more alive to be angry or afraid, and so we don't want to move on from those feelings, not realizing that we can experience alive-ness in other ways.

Grief and pain are not necessarily negative emotions and although they can be difficult, they don't have to be totally unpleasant. There is a sense in which allowing oneself to feel them can be empowering, and therefore on some level enjoyable—or at least they can bring us to joy. Avoiding them or getting stuck in them is a bad idea, but that is true of any emotion. *Fear* of pain or grief is a different matter, and will be unpleasant and disempowering. To be able to walk into a state of grief or pain with your eyes open will allow you to walk right out the other side as the shining being which you truly are.

The labels we have attached to things can limit our understanding of them. When I talk about joy, I don't mean happiness or contentment, although it may include them. I am talking about something very powerful, something that can feel almost ferocious in its intensity. There have been times when I thought I was going to explode with the sensation of beauty occasioned by a particularly stunning sunset.

In this society, we are encouraged to tone ourselves down and be gentle and caring. Yet a powerful sensation may make us enthusiastic, demonstrative, animated, passionate, excited, even to the point of feeling fierce and wild. When our intentions are benevolent, we can allow that without causing any harm to others, although some people may be alarmed simply by an unusually powerful expression of energy flowing. Hopefully, you will know that that kind of alarm is their problem, not yours. And perhaps their alarm is not a problem at all, simply a sign of impending change.

Cultural beliefs

There is a thin line between a feeling of something being wrong, and acting out of insecurities or culturally imposed beliefs. Because most of us want to fit into the society in which we grow up, we have a strong tendency to adopt the beliefs of that society without question. We may be punished and ostracized if we don't. Part of the skill in being human is being able to recognize when a feeling arises out of the fear of being rejected, or out of a personal sense of wrong-ness. Sometimes you may realize that those cultural beliefs are not what you truly believe on a personal level. For instance, if you were brought up in the Moslem faith, surrounded by women with their faces covered in public, you may think that women should always do that. The first time you see a woman with her face uncovered, you may feel shocked—and then you realize you don't want to adhere to the belief that what she is doing is wrong. That belief was imposed on you, and you never previously questioned it. *Many* beliefs are imposed on us by our culture, and when we start to question them, getting to the root of what we personally want in our lives, all kinds of potentials may unfold. The vast majority of people go through life wearing blinders so that they see only within very narrow limits. Another way of saying that is that they are fast asleep. If you want to wake up, you must start questioning everything and looking around you with open eyes. Learn to see beyond the limits imposed externally.

In the end, we are all individuals. You need to develop your own relationship to reality, doing what feels right to you. It doesn't matter if everyone around you thinks you're crazy. That's their problem. The pressure to conform can be very strong, and it requires equivalent strength of character to choose to be who you are if that is different from the norm, but there is no surer way of stepping into your personal power.

The concept of power and trust

It is essential to understand the difference between power over others and personal power. Life force, power, creativity, love, joy— they are all the same thing: energy moving through us. A person who is skilled in the art of being fully alive is allowing the energy to move freely, and can be identified as being in her or his individual power. This kind of personal power is quite different from power-over, which is bestowed by an external source, and involves some kind of hierarchy. People who need power over others make themselves feel greater by putting other people down in one way or another. Personal power is never about other people; it flows from inside out. Someone who is empowered in this way will usually come over as confident, although often quietly so, and self-contained. They don't seek any form of aggrandizement. They are not motivated by an ego need.

How do people become personally empowered? Some people are just born that way. Others develop it through life experience, usually because of events that have led them to a place of self-reliance, where they have learned to allow the energy of the Universe to flow through them, and they have come to accept that a much greater force is taking care of them. They are in touch with a wisdom that flows from inside, so that they know what needs to be done to achieve the desired result. They are in the right place at the right time, without thinking about it. Even when they have apparently missed the boat, fortuitous things happen. They can see what is positive even in dire circumstances. They are in touch with All-that-they-are, and its power. They live in harmony with the energy of the Universe, and it brings to them whatever they need. They are in tune with the unseen rhythm of life. They may not appear to others to be rich, but they experience themselves as rich. They have resolved old feelings and cleared out old energy so that nothing blocks the flow from moment to moment. They are motivated by trust instead of fear, and because they recognize Truth when they see it, they are not easily blinded by delusion or led by others. The light of their own hearts leads them. Of course this state can come and go from to moment. The art of being human is about being able to dwell in that place of centered-ness no matter what is going on around you.

It's quite possible to learn to be in your personal power. It is a feeling of being guided. It requires commitment and a willingness to take risks. Primarily it is about learning to trust in All-that-is, a state that allows the power of the Universe to flow through you.

Trust is a funny thing: you can sometimes trust someone to lie to you, or trust that difficult things will happen. When I use the word, I mean accepting that from a broader perspective, everything is as it should be, in a never-ending process of perfection. Know that there is a much more powerful force at work than we can ever be fully cognizant of, and even when apparently terrible things happen, there is a greater plan. Let go of the ego that wants to control everything, and operate from the heart, from a place of true knowing. That is trust.

Questioning yourself and taking responsibility

In any action you take, your motivation will affect the outcome. Your motivation is about the feeling or thought that prompts you to take certain actions, and the perspective you choose is what will bring up particular feelings. You can change your feelings (or thoughts), and therefore your motivations, by choosing a different perspective. Different perspectives can motivate the same actions, but the ultimate effect of those actions will vary depending on the feeling behind the motivation.

For example, I frequently hear people saying we are destroying this planet. If you believe that, you might consequently decide to recycle, in order to preserve what you see to be dwindling resources. However, if that is your motivation, you are contributing to the planet's destruction, no matter what you are *doing* to contribute to saving the planet. In other words, your experience and interpretation of reality (which is your perspective) has an effect on all of humanity's experience of reality. On the other hand, if you look around you and see evidence that this planet is thriving, and your motive for recycling is the desire to behave respectfully, then you are contributing to the wellbeing of the planet, because you are contributing to a positive perspective on what is occurring around us. This applies to everything. What you are thinking has more effect than what you do.

The Earth is offering us its resources as gifts. When we accept those gifts gracefully, with delight, gratitude, and respect, we are contributing to all life on the planet, because that kind of attitude is one of love. And love is the energy from which all physical things are created. Give abundant unconditional love, and abundance of all things is yours in return. Does this sound too easy? Remember that giving unconditional love requires being fully alive, a choice which may be delightful but also may be terrifying and certainly isn't always easy.

Here is another way of saying the above: motivation for action is always based on a belief (which is what you are thinking) and beliefs carry tremendous energy. The emotion of fear will always produce more negative results than trust. The most beneficial thing you can do for yourself, for everyone else, and for our planet is to develop a positive attitude to life, and act respectfully, which is about being motivated by love. You can transform your fear to love and trust by choosing what to focus on and what to believe. It may require radical changes in your life, but it will certainly make you happier in the long run and that happiness will benefit the whole world.

It is easy to hold a charge about what is going on around you when you feel affected by it. Everyone has their "issues," that throw them into fight mode. Some people like to be in fight mode so that's OK. I don't, because I believe that what I resist persists, and I know how much it exhausts me to be fighting on a regular basis (I spent a lot of my life doing it). I believe I am benefitting this world much more to be celebrating its beauty and alive-ness than mourning for its imminent demise. So I focus on joy, and in general I let others fight their own fights, unless they ask for help.

Understanding how much effect we as individuals can have in the world simply by what we think is sometimes an overwhelming responsibility. I remind you that this is a game we are playing, and we are all doing our best. If you make yourself miserable and weary trying to do the "right thing," you're missing the point. Relax. Enjoy. Appreciate. That's powerful!

Chapter Eight

How to Create in Concrete Reality

"By deliberately directing your attention and thoughts toward
the outcome that you desire, you can be or do or have
anything that you choose." [17]

This chapter is specifically about the process of manifestation, which
might be defined as the art of choice, since it's about how to get what
you choose and choose what you get. Many people immediately think
about manifesting *things*, such as a new car. What I have written
below will help you to do that if you want—and I encourage you to
think very deeply about this. What will ownership of a new car bring
to you? Peace of mind, a sense of satisfaction, a feeling of delight, the
sense that you can keep up with the Jones's? As I have stated already
in this book, the acquisition of things is limited in its ability to fulfill
us. It may be that you are looking for something deeper.

Always bring your desires back to the personal. You may want to
live in a more peaceful world, but changing the whole world has to
start with your personal experience. So state your desire to experience
peace. If your partner is ill, you can manifest the ability to be
supportive and loving, but you cannot interfere with other people's
processes. Everything is about deliberately shaping your self in the
way that you want.

Defining what you want

You don't have to know in advance the details of your new life or
even exactly what it is you want—just stating your desire to have a

---

[17] Esther and Jerry Hicks, *The Astonishing Power of Emotions*. (Hay House, Inc.
2007).

life that delights you is enough. You might decide to get more specific. Is there a quality you want to develop, a feeling you want to predominate in your life, or a thing you want to have? Go to basics. Do you want a better-paid job, or do you want to be appreciated more, or do you want more money? They are three different things. Do you want to be thin, or do you want to be healthier, or do you want to be more attractive to others, or do you want to like your body better? Those are four different things. Perhaps you simply want to live life more fully, feel more confident, or feel less stressed, which you can phrase as feeling relaxed and peaceful, since stating things positively is an essential part of the process. It might be a personality trait you want to let go of; perhaps you want to stop feeling angry. You can think of that as feeling at ease with life, stating that you are now choosing to let your anger pass on.

Consider the ramifications of what you are asking for. Being thin might get you more sexual attention, but loving your body might bring you more happiness and promote good health even if your body isn't picture-perfect according to society's standards. It is a wonderful thing to have enough money, but perhaps the satisfaction you would get from having *more* money won't last long or go very deep. If you primarily want more joy in your life, make that your first priority—you don't need to know how the joy will come; you just need to know you want it.

It is common for people to be seeking a sense of security, which is always elusive, since it's about trying to prevent the inevitable process of change. In reality, what they have to do is to embrace and accept change, living in a state of trust. Decide to manifest a consistent feeling of trust in the process of life.

Once things are rolling, be prepared for unexpected changes to occur, since you will probably find your lifestyle changing as your new of way of being in the world unfolds.

Mistakes are not possible

Be willing to trust that this *can* come about, but don't get stuck in working out how. That's the job of the Universe, and it's not useful for you to try to work things out in advance, because our rational brains can't be aware of all the possibilities. If you put out what you want clearly and don't sabotage yourself, opportunities will begin to present themselves, often in remarkable ways. Then it's up to you to seize those opportunities, and follow through with the ones that are working. They don't all lead directly to what you want—some of them may be more about learning something you need to learn in order to move on, or getting used to new and different experiences.

Don't worry about making a mistake in deciding what you want. You can always change your mind, and it's normal for human beings to change their minds quite often. You will not be stuck with what you get. You can continue to spend your life improving on it. Often we can't know what we really want until we have at least part of it. Then we begin to see more clearly. Or we may come to recognize that our lives are already being orchestrated on a grand scale, and what we think we want changes completely.

Slowing down that ship

No matter what your past has been like, you have the ability to change your future. Don't limit yourself because of what others tell you or because of your past experience, or indeed, for any reason at all. The strength of your desire, or your motivation, is vital, and if you have had a very unpleasant past, your motivation will be very strong, although you may have to be patient. It's like stopping a big ship that is going full speed ahead; it has to finish going that last mile. Then it has to turn around and get up steam to go the other way. It can certainly be done; it just isn't immediate.

Once you are going in the right direction, everything happens faster. The art is not to dwell on the fact that the ship hasn't already changed direction, but to trust that it is going to do so. When you find yourself thinking that nothing has changed yet, then follow up with the thought that the process of change is beginning, and it is going to feel really good when you get to the point of being able to perceive the changes. Many people sabotage their initial choices by giving up too soon, and failing to change the basic internal pattern of expecting things to be in that same old place of lack. There is a great deal of abundance on this planet, and you must learn to perceive it even if it is not in your immediate environment.

Making a commitment

The second step is to commit to what you want without reservation. It is often necessary to give something up in order to move on—and you can't necessarily know what you need to give up until the process is started. You can always change your mind if you find the risk is too frightening, but if you are willing to let go of what is not serving you any more, no matter how comfortable and familiar it is, then it makes room for new and exciting things that *will* serve you. I personally have found that whatever I let go of is always replaced tenfold.

You need to make the commitment full-heartedly, not half-heartedly. State what you want using positive phraseology (no comparatives, no negatives) that feels right to you—remembering that you can always change and improve on it. Write it in an attractive way, because you want to feel pleased every time you look at it. After you have written your statement, write:

I *(your full name)* now commit to whatever
is necessary to allow this desire to manifest.

Sign it, date it, and place it where you will see it, preferably first thing in the morning, last thing at night, and several times during the day. Replace it with an updated version whenever you need to, as things change.

Using your imagination and letting yourself feel

The third step is to let yourself imagine how delighted you will feel when you have this thing, without allowing questions or doubts to creep in. Give your imagination free rein. Let yourself *be* there. Do this for as long as you are able, every day. At first one second may be all you can manage without the doubts coming up. Keep practicing, and soon it will be a full minute. Let the feeling permeate your body, let yourself become aware of the feeling fully throughout your body. Let yourself shiver with delight, jump with joy. Don't censor the way your body reflects the joy of having what you want.

This is a great method for finding things. Say you've lost your wallet. You're wandering around the house fretfully looking for it, and feeling anxious. Stop! Stand still and imagine how good it's going to feel when you are holding your wallet in your hand again. Imagine how relieved you will feel, imagine how it looks in your hand, how it feels on your skin. Let yourself see yourself with your wallet, laughing because after all everything's all right. Now go back to something else—maybe you were checking email or washing up or phoning someone. Distract yourself from the thought of the wallet; you don't need to think about it anymore. You get involved in that something else, and suddenly there is your wallet. Say thanks and get on with your day. While you're at it, you could set the intention of changing the habit of thinking you've lost it. Perhaps you don't need to scare yourself that way anymore.

You can practice projecting positive thoughts in many situations. Perhaps you see a car accident; imagine all the people in the cars involved getting out and walking around unhurt. Or you see a car broken down by the side of the road; imagine the driver starting up and driving off with a big smile. Or you see someone limping; imagine her/him walking normally. Or you are checking out at the grocery and the checker seems really harassed; imagine her/him looking really relaxed.

Paying attention

The fourth step is to pay attention. As you go about your life in your normal way, you will begin to notice unusual things presenting themselves. They may appear to be nothing to do with what you want, but don't ignore them. You may notice things you never saw before, you may find yourself thinking unusual thoughts, or having sensations and feelings that are odd to you. You want to cultivate change, so practice thinking and doing things that are new and different. Have you been in the habit of being suspicious in the past? Let go of that suspicion. If someone smiles at you in the street, smile back. Remember, you are now choosing to be in charge of your own life. Sometimes things will happen that appear to be reinforcing your old habits; perhaps the person who smiled at you starts to harass you because you smiled back. But it is an opportunity for you to respond differently from the way you would have done in the past. Be assertive with the person who is harassing you. Order him or her to leave you alone, without being nasty. And when you think about this situation later on, even if you still think you didn't handle it well, congratulate yourself, knowing that you don't have to feel badly about that other person. There is never any need to blame yourself *or* others when things are difficult. It isn't anyone's fault; it is just a lesson and a learning opportunity. Blaming external sources is a sure sign of unwillingness to take responsibility for your own life, and you must take responsibility if you are going to change. Blaming internal sources (yourself) is being unkind to yourself, and you need to learn to be forgiving of what you might see as your faults.

You may find that the things you want to change come right up in your face once you have decided to change them, as though the Universe is saying, "Are you sure you *really* mean this?" Knowing that you are experiencing the death throes of an old habit, you can choose not to take it all as seriously as you once did.

Being fully present and affirming your choice

If your past has been unpleasant, you may be in the habit of absenting yourself from your life. Now you have to be present. You must start from this present moment, accepting the way things are now, however much you dislike it. Remember, you *are* changing it. It won't always be like this. In order to explore your full potential in life, you need to learn to live every moment fully. You will know that you are present when you find yourself one hundred percent focused on whatever you are doing at any given moment. Incidentally, you will also find that you do whatever you are doing much better, and you will be enjoying doing it well.

Be careful with positive affirmations. People often sabotage themselves by using affirmations that are not true. Don't tell yourself "I experience peace everywhere I go" when you really don't believe that. All that happens then is you throw yourself into conflict and probably get sick. Say instead, "I have started the process of change so that I will experience peace." When you really do believe the process of change has begun, say, "I am beginning to see that peace is all around me." Finally it becomes, "I experience peace everywhere." This is my use of words. You need to choose your own words, the ones that are right for you.

An affirmation is exactly that—it affirms your perception of reality, and in this case, it affirms the fact that you are choosing to change your reality. Language is very important here, on a deep and often subtle level. Every time we say anything, the words we are using are affirming our reality. If you say, "I'm fighting an infection," you are affirming that you are involved in a fight. You might prefer to say, "I'm getting rid of an infection," or "I have had an infection and now it's passing." Watch how frequently you use the words *fight* or *struggle* on a daily basis. Do you want life to stop being a struggle? Are you always talking about what you hate? Inject this statement into your daily vocabulary: "I am choosing to experience ease and abundance." Instead of saying, "This is a struggle," say, "This used to be difficult and now it's getting easier." Over time, that will change to "Life is a delightful process, filled with ease and abundance!"

Saying these statements out loud and breathing deeply as you do so will make sure that you are fully present for the reality of them. But it's also fine to sing positive statements to yourself while you're driving or walking around. You can't say them too often, and singing them is even better.

Addressing habits and patterns of thinking

The fifth step, which is ongoing, is to change your habits of thinking. You must learn to see the glass as half full. You don't label the things you *don't* like as bad, you simply know what feels good to you, and you choose to be where those kinds of things are happening.

You may have to correct the habit of negativity many times a day at first, until you have developed the new habit of positivity. Be patient with yourself. Most people in our world are motivated by fear, and that fosters the experience of fear. You want to foster the experience of trust.

Are you worried about a friend or relative? Worry is a prayer for what you *don't* want. Whenever you find yourself worrying about someone else, visualize that person as the powerful healthy shining being that s/he truly is. *That's* helpful to the person you are thinking about.

Do you want your existing relationship to improve? State your desire to experience it as joyful instead of focusing on what your partner is doing wrong.

Do you want to manifest a relationship with another person? Do you want to be loved? Do things that make you feel loving towards others and everything. The cycle of giving and receiving is essential.

Develop the experience of both, remembering that love is about respect, and that means respecting people's boundaries and differences. Don't impose your ideas on others, no matter how sure you are that you know what they need. Be gentle. Practice experiencing love. In Truth, there is an infinite amount of love available. Feel it from many sources.

Cultivate gratitude and openheartedness. Suppose you live in a place where you often see dog poop lying around. Over time, you get angry with dog owners who don't take responsibility for their dogs. That feeling begins to pervade your vision. One day while you are watching suspiciously, a dog takes a poop, and the dog walker picks it up. You could think, "I bet she doesn't do that every day!" Instead, you call over to her with a big smile: "Thank you for picking it up!"

You have opened your heart, transforming suspicion into joy. Another way of saying the same thing is that you have allowed the energy of joy to flow through you.

Utilizing what sex teaches us

In the process of sexual desire, we experience various stages that might be categorized thus: an initial build-up that demands our attention, an increase in intensity that is a strong physical sensation, a very specific focus, an almost irresistible sense of urgency, and then a powerful and sudden release, followed by a state of bliss which can last a long time if we allow it. In a situation, which we don't define as sexual, these stages can all occur slowly and gradually, but the process may also be rapid, and the format is often similar, with the various states I have described above being more or less acute or prolonged. It may help you to be patient and avoid getting trapped in frustration to identify these different stages of desire as you are going through them. Practice recognizing and savoring these various stages in non-sexual situations, particularly when you are being creative.

The power of manifestation lies primarily in the ability to feel how delighted you will be when you have what you want. That feeling, when it is felt in the body and is not contradicted, *will* bring what you want. Again, you can utilize sex to help you get there. When you are building up to orgasm or you want to have sex and you know it is going to happen, and you feel that delight coursing through your body so that nothing else matters, remember that you can apply this intensity of energy to other situations. When you are in that euphoric post orgasmic phase, and your mind is drifting in bliss land, gently focus it on something you want. No effort needs to be made, just decide and delight.

Being still

We are human beings, not human doings. When we spend our time keeping very busy, we are distracting ourselves from the sometimes-terrifying experience of feeling our feelings and being who we are. Many of us rush around fixing things all day long. It is vital to stop this constant activity. It is a distraction from reality. You need to learn to be still, and allow things to come to you. Your physical self and everything it does is not what does the manifesting, it is the consciousness that you are, that which you truly are. In order to be in a place of wholeness, or integrity, you must develop enough internal silence that you can listen to yourself and to life moving through you. You must allow space for your inner wisdom, which is your own voice, to come through. Staying busy all the time keeps us splintered, separated from Truth. So put away that book, turn off the TV, leave your phone in another room, stop chattering, and sit quietly, watching, listening, feeling, and being.

No doubt you think there are always a million things to be done, and your ego immediately starts getting anxious about them. Just stop. You will be astounded when you realize how little those things matter. You must decide what your priorities are. Do you want to keep on doing life in the same old way, or are you ready to change? Truthfully, getting things done is unimportant. What is important is how you feel.

You may find that your mind runs away with you when you don't stay busy. You don't have to work at keeping it quiet. Just learn to focus elsewhere: on the beauty of the sunset, on a speck of dust glistening, on a tree dancing in the wind, on the color of a billboard. It doesn't matter what you choose to focus on as long as the thoughts that come up as a result don't pull you back into busy-ness or anxiety.

The limits on what we can manifest

Having said that you can manifest anything, I have a couple of cautions. Don't try to change anything too huge. You can't change summer to winter or night to day. And don't try to change anyone else. It doesn't work and it will make you frustrated. You are the only person you can change. You need to work on yourself and your perceptions of reality, which may involve changing your perception that someone or something else needs to be different. Accept the external exactly as it is and look at what you can work and play with internally.

You can develop abilities that are quite unknown amongst "ordinary" people, such as the ability to heal instantly and other activities that are frequently considered miraculous. In Truth, we can do whatever we want. The problem is that when something puts you outside the pale of normal society, you probably have to remove yourself from the normal matrix of belief systems in order to do it. That could be a lonely place. As we embrace the new paradigm, our ideas of what is *normal* will change greatly. In the meantime, be aware that if you start doing miracles, you are likely to be regarded with suspicion.

It takes a certain amount of courage to make changes, since the unknown and unfamiliar often feels a little risky. That point when the ship has stopped but hasn't quite turned around yet can be uncomfortable. And other people's influence can be unhelpful. When you feel discouraged or scared, go back to the sensation of desiring that thing. How much *do* you want this change? That feeling of desire recharges your system. Remember this gets easier and easier the more you do it. Take a realistic look at what you have to lose by trying, and then ask yourself if it's worth it. Perhaps it's not. Perhaps you need some external support. If you don't personally know other people who will support you rather than undermine you (and, sadly, there are people in the world who will undermine you), then at least know that you are not alone in doing this work. In this day and age, millions of people are taking steps to make positive changes in their lives. And we're all rooting for each other.

When it still doesn't work ...

Occasionally we find we simply cannot move on from something we dislike. No matter what we do and how much we practice the above instructions we are still stuck in that job we hate. So I want to mention one other factor here: we have to finish what we've started. No matter how often you tell yourself "I am really done with this job," the Truth may be otherwise—there is something about this job that is demanding to be addressed on some other level. Because you are so busy avoiding the job and refusing to be present for it, you are not getting this thing that needs to be addressed. In this kind of situation, there is only one answer: you have to accept the situation unconditionally as it is, without trying to change anything about it. You must embrace it completely, which means loving it. How you do this is up to you: maybe you focus on the details, you write lists of what you like every day, you acknowledge what it is about the job that benefits you, you admit that you are frightened at the idea of something new and different. Once you are able to embrace the situation, it can come to completion in its own time. Meanwhile concentrate your energy on accepting each moment exactly as it is, without thoughts of the future.

Any time you do something that makes you grit your teeth (or the equivalent) you are in a state of tension, which is a state of resistance. Surrender. It can feel like a tremendous relief when you let go of the outcome you have believed is right. Give in. Give up. Let yourself fall.

You may think giving up is a sign of weakness, but in Truth it requires great courage (which may be motivated by desperation) to surrender completely, to trust that when you stop trying to force things to be the way your rational brain wants, then all will be well.

Eckhart Tolle is an academic who dropped into such an intense state of depression that he came out the other side into a state of bliss—and sat on a park bench doing nothing for months. In *A New Earth*, he says, "The surrendered state of consciousness opens up the vertical dimension in your life, the dimension of depth. Something will then come forth from that dimension into this world, something of infinite value that otherwise would have remained unmanifested."

What you resist persists. Fall back into a place of acceptance, feel the feelings that arise, count your blessings, and enjoy the beauty in this moment. Remember, feelings can pass quickly once you give them some acknowledgment.

Of course, it could be far worse. You might lose a limb, contract a terminal illness, become homeless, be confined to a wheelchair—the possibilities are vast. Instantaneous cures and other miracles certainly can and do occur, but not many of us are able to change when we have reached a desperate state of affairs, and the other influences I have mentioned above may be affecting you more strongly than you can acknowledge on a conscious level. Check the appendix for resources that might be useful in these situations.

Not being attached to outcome

Every day is a new day, and you can allow yourself to be a different person every morning when you wake up. Your friends may find it problematic if you keep changing your mind (or your self); be patient and understanding of that, and still—do what you need to do for yourself. Allowing change on a daily basis is a wonderful skill. You don't have to be the same as you were yesterday.

The stories of what we need and want and what we are manifesting are just the same as any other stories—it's not useful to be attached to them. You must have an idea of what you want before you start the process of conscious manifestation, but life unfolds in mysterious ways, and you need to allow the vastness of being. Don't keep looking for whatever it is you have decided you need. When you keep noticing that it's not there yet, you are promoting the energy of lack instead of the energy of abundance. Appreciate what does come to you, investigate the openings that transpire, be amazed at how complex life is, and what potentials there are that you never saw before. It may well be that you will find some far greater treasure than the one you thought you were going for.

Chapter Nine

Embracing All That Is

"The light streams towards you from all things, all people,
all possible permutations of good, evil thought, passion." [18]

Life is an ongoing process that has no ending. The latest stage in
human evolution is about learning how to accept and embrace the
vastness of being, instead of maintaining a very limited perception of
the nature of reality and trying to control everything with the rational
brain. In this chapter, I am summing up and taking some of these
concepts a little further: clarifying the broader ramifications while
suggesting ways to remain rooted in everyday physical reality.

Being fully alive

Since all energy is life force, it is true to say that being alive is about
allowing energy to move through us. Or we might say that we are
alive because life is moving through us. Fully mastering the art of
being human—that is, being fully in the magnificence of who we
are—is about allowing life to flow through us fully, and it means that
we feel everything fully all the time. That's a lot of sensation. When
we are used to living our lives with limited sensation, it can be very
frightening to feel life suddenly moving through us, and we may
quickly try to quell it, or even think we are ill. I recently met someone
who had an experience of what might be called bliss. His family had
been draining him for many years, while he constantly tried to take
care of them all. One day, he broke down, told them what he thought
of them, and walked out. In doing so, he shed a huge burden—a
weight that was weighing him down. He felt literally lighter, or

---

[18] Rumi, from *The Rumi Collection* by Andrew Harvey, (Shambala 2005).

enlightened. His ecstasy was so unfamiliar that he got scared. Fearing that he might have had some kind of brain tumor, he went to see a doctor.

What an ironic reflection on our society, to be afraid there is something wrong when we feel really good.

However, sometimes the sensation of life moving through us does take some getting used to. Initially, it may feel intolerable to be deeply moved by a perception of beauty that is demanding instant expression. You think you will explode. You want to dance, scream, cry, jump around, or otherwise behave in ways that are unacceptable in many social settings. Question your priorities. Would you prefer to be only half-alive and maintain social etiquette? Or throw all that to the winds and be fully present, fully alive?

Giving and Receiving

The eternal cycle of giving and receiving is an integral aspect of life on this planet, yet many of us participate in it one-sidedly. In order to receive fully, you must be able to give, and in order to give fully, you must be able to receive. Many of us live out our lives without any awareness of the gifts we are being offered from all sides. Following the instructions in this book will enable you to perceive them. Accept them gracefully and gratefully, and utilize them.

For instance, people have told me that my writing is a gift for the world. The way I see it is that I was born with a gift (the ability to write) that demands to be expressed. But I don't write for myself, I write for others, and when others appreciate my writing, it is a gift to me. If no one ever read my writing or benefited from it, I would feel forlorn and unappreciated. I need people to read it, and when they do I am fulfilled, delighted, and very grateful. A necessary part of this is for me to be willing to recognize that I am gifted. Sometimes I have a tendency to belittle my gift, and in effect that belittles other people's appreciation of it, which achieves nothing good. We all need to acknowledge the gifts we bring into this world.

Being endowed with a gift is a responsibility, because all gifts demand to be shared with other humans or with the planet or with some other beings. If your gift is something like finding ease in being alone, it may not appear that it's something you are sharing with others. But the example of you doing what you do affects others, helping them to see what they can do. In the end, the only thing we can offer to the world is ourselves, which includes the gifts we were born with and have developed. In other words, the gift is really just being fully who we are, however that might manifest. Each of us is unique, and we are constantly offering our world the example of our uniqueness.

Life is an endless exchange of love. Delight in that.

Life purpose

These days a lot of people are asking about their life-purpose, which is what All-that-I-am decided it wants to experience in this lifetime before incarnating in this particular body with this personality, these gifts, and these predilections. Sometimes the intention may be as simple as wanting to experience what it is like to be in human form. Someone for whom that is true will probably lead a fairly simple and straightforward life. After a few lives figuring out the basics, maybe we want to experience something more complex: What is it like to be a powerful ruler? What is it like to be a slave? To be disabled? To be a genius? To have a child who dies young? To be ordinary or extraordinary? To be a nun or a monk or an atheist? To be absolutely free? To be deceitful? To be a murderer? To be murdered? To be a drug addict? To live in a very cold climate? To be a musician? An artist? A fighter? A peace-lover? The possibilities are infinite.

In essence, they are all about learning to allow energy to flow freely—or not. At this present time, we as a species are learning how to manifest what we want, which is about playing with energy flows. Many of us have chosen to be born now because this is a particularly exciting time in the evolution of this planet, when all kinds of new possibilities are available to us. We want to participate in the awakening of humanity, which means being able to experience a depth of awareness of reality that was not previously possible.

Commonly, we set some rules for ourselves in each lifetime, such as being compassionate, truthful, independent, or developing some other quality. When we are embodying the quality we have chosen, we feel *right*. When we are acting in ways that contradict it (perhaps because of cultural or familial influences) we may feel confused, unsure of ourselves, anxious, and depressed. We won't feel good. Yet people who haven't made themselves a rule to live in accordance with such intentions will feel fine in the same circumstances that bring up acute discomfort for others. So be careful about looking to others for guidance. Sometimes it can be very misleading. We are all individuals and we are all different.

But it doesn't mean that everything will be easy when we follow our life purpose. We may specifically have chosen all kinds of obstacles, such as social conditioning that makes it difficult. Perhaps we have chosen to participate in expanding the limits of social conditioning, which needs to happen in order to facilitate humanity's awakening, and we need first to learn how to do that for ourselves. Often we choose experiences that are difficult or apparently unpleasant in order to learn certain things. For instance, I chose to experience fear early on in my childhood. Consequently, I have learned a lot about courage. I also experienced sexual abuse, which taught me about personal power and energy flows. Seeing so much denial and cruelty around me as a child has made me choose very consciously to be a truthful and compassionate person.

Everyone's life purpose is about being fully who they have chosen to be in this lifetime, being fully present for life in human form, and enjoying life. However, remember that the concept of joy does not always involve what we consider happiness; it involves fullness of experience.

The meaning of awakening

Awakening is about being very conscious or aware, about refusing to delude oneself, or at least to participate in the delusion that is common on this planet. Consciousness occurs on many levels, and the rational brain cannot possibly grasp more than a small part. In Truth, you cannot do anything without consciousness. There is always some part of you that is aware and conscious. The question is, what part of you was conscious of this, what part of you was not, and is that OK with you? It's certainly possible to learn to be more conscious of what you are doing. You must then take more responsibility for yourself. That requires developing a deeper and broader perspective on what is occurring, perhaps discovering that what we call the *subconscious*, or *unconscious*, is actually in control, whereas what we call *conscious* may refer to only the most superficial level of awareness, where you see only a tiny percentage of what is, and understand only what can be understood with the thinking processes. Being fully conscious is about paying attention to what is really going on, knowing that everything is multi-layered. Many people don't want to take responsibility (that can be hard work and sometimes agonizing), so they carefully, yet *unconsciously,* avoid paying attention to certain things. They don't want to wake up. Let me repeat, that does not mean they are bad or stupid people. They are just choosing a different kind of life from those who are waking up.

So, like everything else, waking up is a choice, often made on a so-called unconscious level. It is not usually the easiest choice, although in my opinion, its rewards are manifold. There is no need to wake people who don't want to be woken, and they won't thank you for trying. Sometimes people are bad-tempered when they first wake up, because it can be quite shocking when they suddenly see things differently, and what they used to enjoy seems inane. They might initially want to go back to sleep, but the process of awakening isn't easily reversible.

The importance of forgiveness

The stories we get attached to are usually about how we were treated badly: by our parents, by someone in the street, by a lover, by a government. The ego loves to explain why life is difficult. When we let go of egotistical explanations and stories, we have to take responsibility for our own lives. We understand that nothing is *done to* us. Everything that occurs does so because we chose it, whether by default or on purpose. There is no longer any external source to blame. The good thing about this is that we are always examining ourselves to make sure we have done our best, and that makes it more likely we will fulfill our potential in life. The bad thing is that we are always examining ourselves to make sure we have done our best, and that can be exhausting. You know that you are letting go of your ego when you look back over your life and want to make amends to everyone you ever hurt in the tiniest way. That's when you must start to forgive yourself.

I have said before that holding onto anything keeps us in a place of suffering. That includes our stories about feeling that we should have done better or that someone else should have done better.

Forgiveness is a way of letting go of the past. When you forgive someone you are not saying that what they did is OK, you are saying, "I'm over it, I'm moving on in my life; this isn't going to be part of my story anymore." Most of us find it more difficult to forgive ourselves than to forgive others, but it is just as important. Let go and move on. Various people have designed great forgiveness meditations that will facilitate this process, see appendix.

Changing our perceptions

I have written about this already but it is important enough that I am writing about it again. There are a million ways to perceive any single thing, and none of them are correct or wrong. What is useful is to be able to perceive everything in a variety of ways so that we can choose whether to focus on it or not, whether it is something we like or not. Even if we decide we really don't like it, there are probably others who do like it, and we must accept that reality even when it seems extraordinary, and even when they are saying they don't like it.

How we perceive things is a personal and individual choice that dictates our attitudes to life. It is about how we create our reality. The way we use words, and the words we choose to use are both a result of our perceptions and also contribute greatly to them. We tend to use certain habitual phrases that perpetuate limited perceptions that our culture accepts without question. We talk about the sun going down, but in truth the sun doesn't go down, the earth has turned away from it. When the clouds cover the sun, we say the sun has gone out. We frequently refer to death as though it is the worst thing that could possibly happen to us, and use all kinds of euphemisms that help to prevent us from accepting it as a normal and necessary facet of life. We speak about fighting illness as though that is a good thing, when in fact accepting it is an approach much more likely to give rise to pleasant results.

Make a habit of watching your words, and practice seeing things differently. See how full and alive this planet is, buzzing with energy that we are normally quite unaware of. When you look at the stars at night, think about how huge the Universe is. It would take a plane twenty-four hours to circle the earth. It would take the same plane three years to circle the largest known star in our galaxy, and there are hundreds of billions of galaxies in our Universe alone. Think about living on a round globe. That has all kinds of ramifications, such as the impossibility of being upside down, or the arbitrary nature of east and west. The study of quantum physics has presented us with many incredible facts about the nature of reality, proving, for instance, that everything consists primarily of space. I suggest that you consider these things with a view to recognizing that the physical reality around us—the simple fact that we perceive some things as solid, for example—is an extraordinary and incomprehensible miracle.

Embracing all that is

If you've read the rest of this book you will know that I'm saying that what you are trying to avoid often will come to you because you are focusing on it. How can you *not* focus on what is around you? How can we focus on the experience of abundance when what we see presently manifesting around us is lack? Here are two separate answers to this question:

1. *Find things to focus on that bring you joy.* You can learn to inhabit your own world even when you are surrounded by people who inhabit a world you don't like. Our perceptions are limited by our culture, which is created by groups of people having the same belief systems and therefore together creating a particular field or matrix or grid of energy. You need to work deliberately and consciously in order to create an energy matrix that is separate from the people around you, not by silencing them or persuading them to change (which would mean you were invested in their energy field), but by establishing and affirming your own beliefs to yourself, and accessing help in that from the Universe— or however the help comes to you. As a result, over time, you will meet other people whose presence feels good to you, and you can mesh your world with theirs. I have found it necessary not to watch TV or read newspapers, and I am careful about what books I read or what movies I watch. I find most forms of media promote limited and negative thinking. I don't want to expose myself to those influences. On the other hand, I find that being alone in natural surroundings is profoundly life-

enhancing, and always leaves me feeling refreshed. Practice spending time by yourself so that you can identify what brings you joy. Best of all is to spend time alone in Nature, since beings in Nature are not trying to impose any beliefs on you.

2. *Learn not to push away the things you don't like.* Make yourself huge so that you contain everything; it flows through you, from your heart or your belly. When you do that, you can turn your attention away from whatever you don't like without labeling anything as bad, and without feeling invaded. Imagine yourself as really vast (which you are); so vast that you contain the whole world. Everything is occurring inside you. I think of it as stepping backwards, or dropping downwards, while an unlimited vastness streams from my heart, embracing everything that I know and everything that I don't know. (After all, you know that all kinds of things you have not personally experienced still exist somewhere.) Within this vastness, I choose where to focus my attention. Embracing everything in this way and allowing it to flow through you is an important tool in dealing with the world. It is an antidote to the sense of overwhelm that occurs when we try to comprehend the vastness of All-that-is with our rational brains. It is a way of allowing a sense of vastness to be with you in your daily life, rather than trying to fit everything into the narrow perspective of reality in which humans normally function.

Embracing everything does not mean that you tolerate anything and everything. If you find yourself surrounded by what you personally dislike, you either change what is going on (by asking others to go elsewhere or stop what they are doing, for instance) or you go somewhere else.

Remember to spend time being still. When you are still, you are not trying to change any of the vast number of possibilities that are occurring around you. You are containing them all, and you are picking out the ones you want to focus on and manifest. When you are being still, you are in a far more effective place of power than when you are running around trying to change things. You are in your personal power.

Doing nothing is one of the most useful activities available to you. Use it. Being active may be fun (and I personally really enjoy it) but getting things done is very unimportant: it is always the process that matters. If it's not a joyful process, what's the point? In any case, the main ingredient for getting anything done is to imagine it done. Don't just *do* something; sit there.

When you embrace everything (All-that-is), allowing it to pour through you, you are at one with everything. You are experiencing one-ness.

Nothing is an accident

Everything that happens is intended and chosen. It may be chosen by default, simply because there may be a lot of fear in our vicinity, and that has to manifest somehow unless it is replaced by a specific individual choosing trust instead. Most of us are vulnerable to the influence of fear.

There is no such thing as a mistake. In fact, it's occasionally necessary to make what you may call a mistake, because it helps us to clarify what we want and what we don't want—the first essential ingredient of choice. Mistakes enable us to discover things we wouldn't otherwise be consciously aware of.

It may seem overwhelming to imagine the level of organization that is constantly occurring in order for everything that happens to be intended. And it also may seem very odd that the Universe (which is you) intends some of these things. Why would anyone intend to contract cancer, have a car accident, get beaten up? Remember that they are chosen from a perspective where there is no time, where death and illness are merely aspects of life, and pain is not differentiated from pleasure. The art in relating to unpleasant occurrences with equanimity is about stepping back into that perspective, and seeing the terrifying magnificence of All-that-is.

Recognizing that there is no such thing as an accident means seeing that there is a purpose in everything. You might have an accident or get sick when it is time for you to die, or you could choose either of those as a way of reminding yourself that you want to be fully alive. You might get beaten up because you need the experience of being at someone else's mercy, because you need to move to a different neighborhood, because it brings up feelings that must be addressed, because of past karma, because there is something in your life that you are trying to avoid, because it will help you to develop compassion, or any one of many other reasons. It might be a shortcut to something that would otherwise take lifetimes to learn. If you don't want to repeat that lesson, you will have to allow yourself to experience all aspects of it.

Any time things don't work out the way you planned them, look at what is being offered and required. What is this for? How can this serve you and the higher good? What is the meaning behind this? What are you being shown? Sometimes we cannot divine the meaning because other things must first unfold. Learn to trust that there is a grand plan, and that you have a place in it. You could not have been born if you did not have a place in it. Nothing is incidental.

Because we are so effectively forgetting who we are, we have forgotten that it is we who create this planet and everything on it. We have made up a million reasons to explain why things are the way they are: genetics are at the root of all kinds of problems, global warming is changing the climate, political power struggles use us as pawns, bacteria cause disease, and so on. Stop using these excuses. See everything that happens as part of a grand experiment in being human and in forgetting that we create all this from moment to moment, by choice. We have chosen it to be this way. At first you may be appalled when you begin to see what we have chosen. After a while, it becomes amazing, extraordinary, magnificent, and only a little terrifying.

When you recognize that we are the ones doing the choosing, you have to take responsibility for your choices, and if you are anything like me, you often ponder why you have chosen something that does not appear to be fun. You always discover a reason sooner or later. From the perspective of the vastness of the consciousness that we are, things look pretty different and the world runs on different priorities.

Self-empowerment versus self-delusion

Acknowledging that you are constantly choosing what is occurring around you is profoundly self-empowering, because you realize that you can create your reality and you don't have to partake in cultural delusions. Once you truly accept that the world is only dangerous for those who believe that it is dangerous, you can begin to replace that belief with one that you prefer. It's not necessarily easy to do, because these are beliefs we grew up with, that are embedded deep in our subconscious. We can't just decide in our conscious minds not to hold these beliefs anymore, because that is not where the beliefs reside. And you cannot pretend to change a belief. Pretense doesn't work when you are operating from a place of Truth—and you will be doing that when you allow life to move through you. (This may be alarming for people who have spent all their lives presenting an image that isn't true.)

Make sensible choices about what to do with yourself and where to place yourself on this planet related to what you are intending. If you want to experience the world as a safe place, it would be counter to that intention to hang out where there is a lot of evidence that the world is a dangerous place. Some people like challenges, and they may give themselves a challenge in many ways: getting into debt so that paying the bills every month is difficult, for instance, or living in a city where there is a great deal of crime. It's fine to choose these kinds of challenges unless you really want a life of peace and ease, in which case you will find those challenges very unpleasant. They may have been things you did in the past but now that you are being real, honest, and realistic with yourself, you are not willing to tolerate them anymore. You no longer want to play those particular games.

When you step out of the state of self-delusion and start being really truthful, examining and accepting your true motivations and desires, you may discover aspects of yourself that you don't like. Remember that trying to change something is similar to resisting it. Allow it instead, even if you dislike it. It already exists right now, after all, and you cannot make it *not* exist right now. Embrace it all in the vastness that you are: the fact that there is this aspect to your self, and the fact that you dislike it. Disliking an aspect of your self does not mean you dislike your self. Respect and appreciate the complexity of this body and personality that you have chosen, knowing that it is constantly changing. Have you decided that you want to manifest compassion? Then you are in the process of learning how to do so. Focus on that. In the meantime, now and always, be patient and kind with your self.

Human evolution—beyond survival

The process of human evolution—that is, integrating a deeper and broader awareness of the nature of reality into our daily lives—is ongoing, and recently it's picked up a surge of speed. Many of us are awakening, choosing to live intentionally and harmoniously. We are moving beyond the limited thinking that arises out of what I call a survival mentality. Many of us are no longer stuck in a place where we struggle to find enough food and shelter. We have decided to move on from that paradigm and we are shifting our energy. This is happening on a global level and it's a wonderful thing. However, part of what we are seeing around us is polarization. The divisions between people still in survival mode and those not in survival mode are getting clearer. This has nothing to do with how much money you have in the bank, or how big your house is, or even whether you have a house or not. It has to do with how much you trust that you are provided for. When you trust in All-that-is, when you know that all is well, amassing money or possessions is incidental.

It may be unpleasant seeing this global polarization, and you may think that it is your job to help others wake up. In Truth, if people don't want to wake up, it is kinder to leave them asleep. They are perfectly happy being asleep. If you don't perceive them as perfectly happy, that may only be because you have a specific definition of what happiness looks like. Some people have to have something to complain about in order to feel happy, and so you are not doing them a favor in trying to remove the reason for their complaints.

Respect, violence, and truth

How would it be to know that everything in the world is absolutely as it is intended to be, and nothing needs to be changed? Sit with that awareness. Know that nothing is wrong, and you are not trying to change anything, because nothing needs to be changed. There is no need to be annoyed with yourself for failing in any way because the concept of failure is basically flawed. Everything is perfect in this moment. Time is unlimited. The possibilities of life are unlimited. Our resources are also unlimited (however much our limited vision tells us otherwise). At the same time everything is changing, and things are constantly passing. We tend to get anxious with this constant change and often we try to prevent it, which is not only hopeless, but also means we are choosing to be stuck—the source of suffering. Embracing change is the best thing we can do for ourselves and for the world around us.

But, since everything is fine the way it is, does that mean that we can use our resources thoughtlessly, creating lots of waste without bothering what happens to it? No, certainly not. There is no value in worrying about the future, and it is very important to develop a positive attitude. However, it is essential that we learn to act with respect at all times, in relation to all things: other beings and the Earth herself. How we choose to be in the world is what we will experience, and if we treat others with disrespect, we will experience disrespect.

Respect is a specific way of being, and it requires acting in accordance with Truth. The diversity of life is to be honored. Other people's choices are what they are, and we must accept them, no matter how blind and foolish we think they are. That may mean *not* helping someone, even someone who appears to be asking for help, if that person is not ready to change. People sometimes ask for help when they really just want attention. In Truth, you will always know when a person is genuinely asking for help. We are often misled by wanting any or all of the following:

- To alleviate apparent suffering, since most of us find it acutely uncomfortable to watch someone in pain;
- To feel like you are a do-gooder, since the ego is often deeply relieved when it thinks it has done something useful; and
- To be seen by others as a good and useful person, which can bring all kinds of superficial benefits.

Being attached to the label "good" lays the groundwork for a lot of denial. Good people are not supposed to like fighting and violence, after all. Yet the great majority of human beings are

103

fascinated by violence, physical and otherwise. The popularity of violent TV shows and sports that often result in injuries are the most obvious evidence of this obsession, but here are a few other examples: feeling savage delight when someone gets their comeuppance; making snide comments that are intended to put someone down; bitching about the neighbors/the in-laws/the kids, or anyone else; snarling at another driver on the road; yelling at the dog; craning to see an injured person who has been in an accident. The variations are infinite. Many of these may appear so minor that you discount them, but they all reflect a certain attitude.

There is nothing wrong with any of that. It doesn't make you bad if you have a secret (or not so secret) enjoyment of violence, and it doesn't make you good if you don't. Those labels simply become meaningless. However, if you are pretending to abhor violence, that pretense will sap your energy, and things that are kept secret tend to fester. You can roll your eyes and shake your head, and still admit what is true. When you openly acknowledge your interest in violence, at least to yourself, you can make sure to express it in harmless ways, without lashing out at others or yourself. Turning a violent tendency inwards may be more socially acceptable and less obvious, but it has negative effects in the long run. Sadly, it's habitual for many people. It's a very disrespectful way to treat yourself. You may think that's better than being disrespectful to others, but the long term result is that you will need others to take care of you as you deteriorate due to lack of love from the inside.

I sympathize with parents who want to teach their children to shun violence. Yet, if a child is allowed to indulge in violent fantasies as much as she wishes, she will eventually tire of violence on a deep level, and genuinely choose peace instead. If the child feels he must pretend to loathe violence, he is much more likely to harbor a hidden fascination, as many of us do.

We commonly spend a great deal of energy trying to justify ourselves in our own eyes and in the eyes of others. We make up rationalizations that are half-truths, or sometimes outright lies, and the more convincing they sound, the more relieved we feel, thinking we have successfully avoided a negative judgment (and we have at least avoided our own). Why go to so much bother when the net result is you are not fully in alignment with Truth? Wouldn't it be easier to let go of the judgment that arose in the first place? We humans take life too seriously. We need to learn to laugh at the extraordinary paradox of being human.

Self-care versus selfishness

I have mentioned the importance of taking care of yourself and paying attention to your inner wisdom, which always tells you what you need and what is right for you. A great deal of the skill in being human is about trusting your own inner knowing, and learning not to be affected by the three motivations I have mentioned above. They are powerful influences for most people, especially women. We make it a priority to help others, relegating our own needs to the back burner, which in effect means that we are being disrespectful to ourselves. You may think that you are bringing joy to the world by helping others, but if it means that you are not taking care of yourself, that joy will always be diluted by the negative effect on your own being, however that may manifest: illness, depression, or irritation, for instance. When you help others from a place of joy, in the absolute certainty that this is what you desire to be doing right now, *then* you are manifesting ease and delight for everyone. Indeed, you don't need to *do* anything in order to help others if you are in a place of joy, because joy is infectious and your presence is all that is required for it to spread. Those who are ready to be in joy themselves will quickly follow your example. Those who can't go there yet may still be influenced by your example.

So even though it may sometimes be very difficult, it is important to learn to say no gently and clearly instead of being pulled off-balance trying to fulfill external demands that do not bring you pleasure. Pay attention to that tiny voice inside which you have been taught to silence.

Of course, this can lead to selfish behavior, and there is a fine line between selfishness and self-care, or self-love. The former comes from a place of ego that is unhealthy and the latter comes from a place of individuation that incorporates an understanding of oneness. Or you can put it this way: the former arises out of fear of lack and a sense that there is not enough, while the latter arises out of trust in abundance and a self-awareness that comes from a deep place of love for all things. One is competitive and the other is cooperative.

We all need love, and we can learn to let it flow from inside. Sometimes you can form a partnership with another person, or people, where you give each other the love and attention you need, but the downside of that is that you become dependent on that other person, and she or he may not be there forever. It is better to learn to receive love first from that internal source that is available to all of us, and then form healthy partnerships that don't involve dependence, but support change and growth. Taking responsibility for fulfilling your own needs frees you up to love someone else unconditionally.

A changing world

The electro-magnetic grids that we are part of, which we can feel but cannot see, are changing. So, although we may get a strong sensation that everything is different, there is often no apparent evidence of it, and people still go on behaving in the same old ways, and then being surprised because things don't work the way they used to. Be willing to do things differently even if you have no external reason to do so.

These changes may manifest in the physical body as strange pains or discomfort that come and go quite fast. Remember that pain doesn't always mean something is wrong. They might just be growing pains. Don't rush to a doctor. Don't try to fix everything that is uncomfortable—sometimes it's necessary to sit with what's going on and allow it to resolve itself over time. It is especially important to understand this if you are in any of the healing professions, since people may come to you with unusual symptoms that don't conform to standard diagnoses. Surprising treatments may be called for, while sometimes reassurance and patience are the answers. Listen to your inner wisdom, however odd the information you are given may appear to be.

Never forget the power of intention and the availability of help. Set your intention to allow shifts to occur with ease, and ask for help when you feel uncomfortable.

In the new paradigm, all kinds of things that we once could not imagine or thought were impossible (such as the Internet) are becoming available to us. Be willing to let go of what no longer serves you even if it feels safely familiar. Stride into the unknown with your heart leading the way. Don't limit yourself with old beliefs that no longer apply. Humanity's potential is very exciting.

Beyond duality

When we wake up, we are able to see existence in a different way. We begin to perceive the inner songs of all the different forms of life. You don't need to hear this with your ears; you hear it with your heart. You feel a rhythm around you, inviting you to partake in the delightful dance of life. You move in harmony with Nature, where beings exist in a pure vibration of being. Unlike many human beings, they are not trying to pretend to be other than they are.

Beyond duality, everything is love. It is all there is. Creativity— everything that is created—arises out of love. Now, the obvious question is, how can everything be love when there is so much cruelty and violence?

Think of it like a loaf of bread. If you were from another planet and I showed you a loaf of bread, telling you it is the same stuff as a field of wheat, you might disbelieve me. There isn't much reason why you should believe me since there is no apparent similarity between a loaf of bread and a field of wheat. That's what love is like— sometimes hard to recognize. Have you ever seen a cat playing with a mouse? The cat really loves that mouse. Love is motivating the cat to play with the mouse in a way that will inevitably injure it. As adult civilized human beings, most of us like to think we would never do that, but children still frequently damage things that interest them. It's part of their process of growth. Even some adult civilized human beings behave like that; considering the prevalence of domestic abuse, perhaps many do.

While still in human form, we can experience a state beyond duality where love, truth, beauty, delight, bliss, peace, and one-ness are all the same thing. This kind of love is different from loving your partner, although it may include that. It is vast and unconditional. Experiencing this is not something that can be taught. In the end, you must simply intend to experience it. When we are fully in this state of one-ness, labels seem meaningless, so we cease to apply them. That means we stop being judgmental, and we may no longer be appalled by things we once thought were awful. We might then appear to other people as callous. This, of course, often prevents people from staying in that state of one-ness; they want to revert to being socially acceptable, and having socially acceptable points of view. I'm not saying that one state is better than the other. I am suggesting that you watch your self, so that you can make clear choices rather than falling by default into certain habits of being.

Human life is full of paradoxes, and as we go through various stages of awareness, which can happen very fast, we get different reactions from people around us. Learn to let those reactions come and go, knowing they have little to do with you. They are a sign of someone else's state of being. In other words, what someone else thinks of you says much more about that person than it does about you.

Chapter Ten

My Own Story

I was born in Scotland in 1952, in a repressed, rural, alcoholic, agnostic setting. I went to church a few times with my grandmother and figured it was pretty silly. I always knew that something was missing from the world around me, without having any idea what that something might be. In later years, I realized that the missing piece was about Truth. The people surrounding me were in serious denial and were invested in telling consistent lies so that they could remain in denial. I struggled without success to make sense of the lack of congruency around me. I spent a lot of time playing alone in the woods, which was greatly preferable to my home life, and I formed a strong, deeply loving relationship with Nature, which enabled me to survive.

In my late teens I attended university in England to study biology. The course included a short class on ecology, which, in the early seventies, was not a word that many people knew. My studies persuaded me that our constant progress was destroying the world, and being someone who never does things by halves, I decided I wanted no part in it. I dropped out, becoming a hippie, a radical activist, and one of the first environmentalists, living in a commune and smoking a lot of hashish. Determined to learn how to live independently of the large corporations, I worked for a year on an organic farm run by John Seymour who was the guru of self-sufficiency in the UK at the time. Realizing that in order to run a farm it would be helpful to know some basic mechanics, I took a government training course in Agricultural Machinery Maintenance and Repair. I was the only woman who had ever done this course, and my fellow students were not friendly to me, to put it mildly. Feminism was sweeping through the Western world; I embraced it with ardor, and came out as a lesbian, which in the seventies was no easy thing. In many ways it felt like coming home, but the lesbian community in the UK was rife with inner conflict that tore it apart as women began to speak their minds and release their anger for the first time in centuries. During those years, I was a committed activist in a number of arenas, and narrowly avoided spending time in jail. I lived as true to myself as I could, but I was fighting my way through a fog. I felt like an outsider on the far reaches of social acceptance, and the times when I experienced the presence of kindred spirits in human form were regrettably rare. At least my political activities gave me an outlet for my frustration and an excuse to fight, which was at that time very empowering for me on a personal level.

In 1982, deeply disillusioned both with the levels of sexism I encountered in England and with the lack of integrity amongst my supposed allies, I moved to northern California, where I worked as a carpenter, living in the boonies. Life here was much easier for me, both as a lesbian and as a woman in manual trades, than it had been in the UK. I had the luxury of space away from political activities and constant conflict. I had plenty of time on my own to think about what I really wanted on a personal level. Once I'd run an organic market garden and built my own house out of recycled lumber, I began to look for something deeper than superficial achievements and possessions.

At that time in California, as opposed to Britain, it was much more acceptable to do introspective work on one's *stuff*, and I embarked on a healing odyssey precipitated by ongoing anger that seemed to have no relationship to my present life. I recalled being molested and abused as a kid, which was a great deal of the source of my anger. I started shamanic work, which I found powerful, and did a one-year training in Angeles Arrien's Four-Fold Way, which enabled me to move on from my father's negative influence. All this required a lot of introspection. I also started doing Wiccan ceremonies, which are about being in tune with the Earth. Since I already felt a strong bond with Nature, this made a lot of sense to me.

In my forties, at a retreat in Montana with Brooke Medicine Eagle, I met Dayana Jon, who is a visionary and the medium for the group of beings called AMAG. The first time I saw her go into trance, allowing them to come present, I experienced the room filling up with love and wisdom. Because that was such a strong physical sensation, I trusted it completely. Over the next ten years, I slowly got to know Dayana and did some workshops with AMAG that were profoundly eye opening. I have met and worked with a few other psychics, but none have been as delightful as Dayana and AMAG.

At the same time, over a period of years, I did a lot of work on healing my childhood traumas around sex. I began to grasp that sex is a powerful tool, one that is consistently ignored, distorted, and misunderstood in Western culture. That motivated me to write *When the Earth Moves*, which has been reprinted as *The Ultimate Guide to Orgasm for Women*. I am happy to say that book has been and still is helpful to many people. I wanted to take those concepts to another level, which is partly what this book is about.

In 1999, I met a woman from Seattle who is a shamanic practitioner and a psychic healer. I wrote a book about her (*With the Sun in My Eyes*), which gave me an excuse to follow her around for months and ask as many questions as I wanted. I also interviewed a number of other psychics for another book I intended to write. All this research helped me to understand more and more about the many realms that we cannot see.

At this point in my life I was seriously tired of fighting and recognized that fighting for peace is nonsensical, but I still felt a deep dissatisfaction that wasn't being addressed. In my late forties, after being diagnosed with hepatitis C, I was hounded by the questions: *Who or what am I? Who put me here on Earth, and why?* I asked everyone from Buddhist teachers to shamanic workers to ordinary people in the street, and not one of them gave me any kind of answer that made sense to me. AMAG was useful, mostly by asking me questions that helped me to broaden my perspective on human existence. One day, feeling very refreshed after talking with them, I left to drive across the mountains.

I was deeply pleased with the world. At some point, this sensation of pleasure became all that I am, all that is. I stopped the car and got out, turning round and round, staring in astonishment at the trees and the road, at the passing cars and the sky. Something truly indescribable (existence itself, perhaps) was occurring.

Of course, now that I have said it was indescribable, I am going to try to describe it.

Everything around me was breathtakingly beautiful. The air was suffused with golden light, and I was lit up by that light. I was breathing it, as it breathed me. I felt it filling me up, creating me. I was transported, de-lighted, and completely at peace. I desired nothing. The vastness of that moment, which was always, was all I could possibly need or want. I understood that *all is well*. Whatever I might have thought to be the meaning of those words, I had not understood them before this moment. There was no possibility that anything could be wrong. Even if there were a major accident and bodies were strewn all over the road, I would still know that all is well. This knowing astounded me. It moved me in a way I had never been touched before, in some very deep place where I am beyond human.

This is how it always has been and always will be.

Like that blissful aftermath of orgasm, the knowing faded over a few days. I did what we humans are so good at: I fell back into a kind of sleep where I layered reality with an illusion that is delightful, appalling, terrifying, compelling, and above all, familiar. It's called daily life.

What I did remember is this: that no matter how I might feel in any given moment, there is the possibility of existing in a place of peace that is far beyond any concept of peace and war. When I am in that place of awareness that all is well, I am more powerful than I could ever know, without even caring about the concept of power. Anyone who comes into contact with me at those times is bound to experience my vastness, which is a much more effective way to initiate change than any kind of fighting.

No *having* or *doing* can be as profoundly effective as being in that place of peace.

A few months later, I was driving in the city, maneuvering my truck through the traffic, trying not to feel enraged with drivers who wouldn't get out of the way, when I found myself thinking, *there must be an easier way to get from A to B*. A month or two later I had the opportunity of asking AMAG this question. Their response was:

"Well, you have thought yourself here, you can certainly think yourself somewhere else! You believe that you require muscular or mechanical means to move yourself around, but in fact all movement occurs because you think it."

A long conversation ensued, leaving my mind reeling. What I did understand is that my body and everything else I experience are thought forms created by me. Therefore, what I think and what I believe are very important, and not static, but changeable.

I wanted to utilize this magnificent power of thought consciously. When I asked AMAG how to learn this, they said, "You only have to choose it."

I made a decisive commitment, to whomever one makes such commitments: *I will do whatever it takes to let go of all my old limiting belief systems. I am nearly fifty, I've tried many things in my life, and now I want something real.*

Soon after this, I was riding my horse late on a December afternoon. I have no memory of what occurred, but I must have fallen off and lain unconscious on the ground for an hour or two. Gradually, piece-by-piece, I became aware of physical reality. It was completely dark, I was extremely cold, and excruciating pain was emanating from the area of my head. I couldn't make my body work properly. I had no awareness of who I was, why I was there, or where I was. That stuff wasn't important. I just knew that this body felt very bad and needed help. Making out the shape of a vehicle parked close to where I was lying, I figured that meant there would be people nearby who could help me. I managed to crawl over to the vehicle and pulled myself upright. When I opened the door, a smell of mold hit me and I suddenly remembered who and where I was. I knew that this vehicle was the old abandoned truck parked down my driveway, which meant the closest inhabited house was half a mile away by road, or a very steep walk through the woods. Both were impossible on a dark, moonless night, considering I couldn't stand up without support. All this flashed through my brain in a split second.

The next thing I remembered was lying on the floor in the house half a mile from where I had fallen. The owner had covered me with blankets and called an ambulance. Later, she told me I fell in the door of the house and crashed to the floor. How did I get there? Since I had not a scratch or a bruise on me, it's impossible that I walked or crawled. Did I create this whole scenario because I wanted to have the experience of moving myself by the power of thought, and I could only do that when I'd hit my head hard enough to displace all the old belief systems about needing muscles or mechanics to get from A to B?

An ambulance took me to the hospital. Once I was warm enough, and had ingested a painkiller to calm my throbbing head, I felt quite happy, in a way that was quite unfamiliar to me. For the next few days, I simply sat, observing and appreciating what was around me. I wasn't at all bothered about anything. The list of things-to-do that normally started my day didn't even cross my mind.

Everyone else was worried that I would die because I had serious concussion. Over the next few days, dealing with their anxiety, I realized that avoiding death was not a motivation that carried any clout with me whatsoever. I was only concerned about enjoying life.

Three days later, I was back to my normal physical state, carrying on with my life the same old way. Three months later I got a mysterious illness. For nine days I lay in bed, alternating between such a high temperature that I soaked the sheets in seconds, and such a low temperature that I couldn't get warm with ten thick blankets on the bed. I refused to go to hospital, knowing that what I was going through was a result of my decision to change my life. It was a healing crisis, a cleansing of old outmoded stuff. It needed to be allowed. At that period in my life, I was writing a book about a shamanic practitioner from Seattle. She and a friend did some shamanic work to help move things along. Still, it was six months before my energy fully returned.

So I spent a lot of the spring and summer lying around. I was still hounded by questions such as, *who or what am I, that I can create myself through the power of thought? What are the limits on this potential?*

In a consultation with AMAG, they told me, "The illness you have created is a little like an incinerator, which is used to dispose of thoughts and feelings that are no longer useful, or healthy, so that *the you* that you are and have always been, emerges. You may benefit from looking at your eyes in a mirror, so that you can feel who is looking back at you."

When the conversation was over, I went into the bathroom and looked in the mirror, thinking I would stare soulfully at myself for a few minutes. As I glanced into my own brown-green eyes, surrounded with wrinkles, I met myself, again. I was so intensely shocked that I actually jumped backwards. In that instant, I vividly recalled the last time I met myself, an occasion that I had dismissed as a nightmare. This is the memory that came to me: I was seven years old, lying in bed one night, when I became aware of the air in the room vibrating. At first it was quite slow, then the vibration gradually speeded up. As it became faster and faster, I found myself having trouble breathing. Soon I could barely make my lungs expand. My breath got shorter and shorter until I was gasping for air, thinking I would certainly die. Just as the terrifying feeling of suffocation engulfed me, I managed to make myself leap up and dash for the window. I thrust my head outside, taking great gulps of air, which somehow brought back the ability to breathe normally, although the air outside was no different from the air inside.

Shaken though I was by this memory (something I hadn't thought about for many years), I continued to look into those eyes. The being I saw looking back at me was certainly not human and not the kind of being you would want to mess with. It was all-powerful, all-knowing, and vast beyond any mental comprehension. It was implacable, determined, absolutely focused, and quite unmoved by considerations of pain or grief. How do I know this? The same way I knew peace on the drive to Seattle. The same way I know my name. The same way we know all things.

After perhaps ten seconds, the sensation of this unthinkable presence faded away, and I was just looking at myself in the mirror.

But isn't that what I was doing all along?

It took me weeks to process the magnitude of this experience. The word that came to me, to describe the being-that-is-me, is *ruthless*—an interesting word, literally meaning *without rue*, which means *without regret*.

Now I had the answer to the question that had hounded me, *Who am I?* And I know now that, since that's the kind of being I am, there is never the slightest reason for me to be afraid of anything. I might experience some things as unpleasant, and choose not to repeat them but All-that-I-am cannot be harmed. This doesn't mean I don't get afraid, but I am usually (not always) able to differentiate a realistic fear—of being run over by a car when I step in front of one, for instance—from an unrealistic one.

Later, AMAG told me that the experience of dying is often one of suffocation, because it requires concentration on the part of spirit to pump air into lungs, and when spirit removes that focus, then the physical being cannot get enough oxygen to continue living. The *dream* I had when I was seven years old occurred because I had begun to let go of my human identity/body, intending to die. Then I met my Self and understood the vastness of being, which made me decide to continue in human form after all.

After all these experiences, I sold my house and most of my possessions because I wanted to live in joy on a daily basis, which meant that I had to stop my habitual busyness and experience absolute freedom. I couldn't see any other way of doing that without changing my life quite radically. Over the years, being a practical person, I'd cultivated an image of myself as someone who fixed things, and that came from a shallow egocentric place. I needed to move on from this identity, to stop being useful, and just be me. I took to the road, going wherever I felt called at any point in time. For several years, I spent a lot of time alone in the wilderness, away from people, which enabled me to establish a deep and loving connection with what is unseen, and to work very specifically with the power of my thoughts.

Over time, I felt called to come back into the world, participating in the awakening of humanity and taking part in the huge shift that is occurring. I wrote a great deal and started teaching shamanic journeying, which is a great way to access the vastness of being. I continue to study with AMAG, who are endlessly helpful. I still travel constantly, mostly living in my vehicle. I took up kitesurfing as an outlet for my physical energy. That dance with the water and the wind is a deeply rewarding pastime that leaves me in a place of joy, with a profound awareness of the importance of being. Everything that is false falls away. Today, even though I know that my coaching and writing are important, I still feel that my greatest value is the joy and clarity that I bring to the planet when I dance with the wind.

A brief one-page primer on the rules for being fully alive and creating the kind of life you want:

➤ Open your eyes and really look at what is around you. See with your heart. Feel what is right and wrong for you personally, without the judgments that normally cloud our perceptions.

➤ Make friends with your Self, your Body, and All-that-you-are. Accept and listen to your body and the messages it is offering you. Act with respect towards your Self and everything/one else.

➤ Choose and commit. Make decisions. What are your preferences in this life? Learn to be optimistic and focus on what brings you joy. Be proactive.

➤ Allow energy to flow through your body, expressing itself in whatever way is required. Rejoice in that, moving beyond the limits of social convention. Be enthusiastic and demonstrative.

➤ Trust in the process of life unfolding, and be willing to change every day. Ask for help, accept it, and express your gratitude. Feel. Touch. Delight. Laugh. Breathe. Cry. Dance. Sing. Run. Love.

♥ Appendix ♥

The following is a short list of resources. In these days of easy Internet access, I recommend you use a search engine for the most up-to-date information. I have mentioned some specific book titles and URLs, but my intention is only to give you somewhere to begin, trusting that what you need will present itself once you undertake the search.

Dayana Jon and **AMAG** are my favorite teachers. They offer public discussions (in person or via teleconference), private consultations, and study courses. You can listen to some past conversations on Dayana's website, www.dayanajon.com.

Abraham is channeled by **Esther Hicks**. She and her husband have produced several books and many recorded conversations, talking a great deal about manifestation in terms that most people can understand. Esther travels a great deal, doing public conversations.

Jane Roberts, who channeled an entity called Seth in the sixties and seventies, has been dead more than thirty years, but her writing has influenced many people. The written material from Seth is still available and still relevant.

Carlos Castaneda was an anthropology student in southern California in the sixties and seventies. He studied with a Mexican sorcerer (or shaman) called Don Juan and wrote a series of books about his experiences. The books are still worth reading, although the emphasis tends to be on battles with other sorcerers. I am more interested in a path of love.

Professor Brian Greene is an American theoretical physicist and string theorist. The PBS special, *The Fabric of the Cosmos*, which features him, is well worth seeing, and he has also written a number of books very accessible to the ordinary non-scientist. He has a wonderful ability to present complicated theories of quantum physics in terms laypeople can understand.

Dr. William Tiller (www.tiller.org) is Professor Emeritus at Stanford University and a pioneer in the study of psychoenergetics, a term used to describe the use of the conscious mind to manipulate matter and energy in order to achieve a particular result. Tiller appeared in the movie, *What the Bleep Do We Know?*

Dr. Jill Bolte-Taylor is a brain researcher who had a massive stroke that enabled a blissful experience of existence beyond the arena of the rational brain for a brief period. Her talk on TED about that is fascinating, and she has also written about it in her book, *My Stroke of Insight*.

Dr. Micheál Ledwith is a disillusioned Catholic priest who addresses existential questions like, *Who are we? Where did we come from?* He has investigated the phenomenon of orbs in great detail, and has some fascinating theories about them. You can access his DVDs at hamburgeruniverse.com

Zechariah Sitchin, who died in 2012, was an academic who spent his life studying many of the scientific anomalies that other scientists carefully ignore. His most well-known theory (supported by a surprising amount of archeological evidence) is that the Greek gods were visitors from another planet. He has written many books, most notably *The 12th Planet*.

Joan Ocean leads seminars, takes people swimming with dolphins (in an absolutely natural setting), and has some interesting things to say about **orbs**, other **dimensions**, and **Bigfoot/Sasquatch**, with whom she communicates regularly.

Stephen and **Ondrea Levine** are pioneers of conscious dying. Their books include *A Year To Live, Who Dies?* and *Healing into Life and Death*.

Jack Kornfield, also an author and a contemporary of the Levine's, does similar work with more of a Buddhist tinge. His **forgiveness** meditations are profound.

Eckhart Tolle has written a number of books and been featured on Oprah. His is best known for writing *The Power of Now*.

Jan Frazier was a fairly ordinary middle class white American when she experienced an extraordinary transformation. *When Fear Falls Away: The Story of a Sudden Awakening* (Weiser Books, 2007) is her day-by-day account of the shift in consciousness and its alteration of her life.

Byron Katie is author of several books (*Loving What Is; I Need Your Love: Is That True?* and others), and leads workshops all over the world in what is called "The Work." It's all about questioning yourself and getting down to what is really true. A lovely being, a wonderful teacher.

Pema Chödrön is a Western Buddhist teacher whose writings speak to many Westerners looking for ways to navigate difficult emotional terrain.

Jean Slatter is author of *Hiring the Heavens*, a simple and straightforward guide to accessing help from other planes of consciousness. She offers workshops on opening to the fullness of being and an online course in becoming a Certified Higher Guidance Life Coach.

Don Miguel Ruiz is a Mexican author and a modern day shaman of the Toltec lineage. He has written several books, most notably *The Four Agreements* and *The Mastery of Love*. His views on how our belief systems limit us and how to get beyond them are very useful.

Angeles Arrien, PhD., who died in 2014, was a cultural anthropologist. One of the spiritual leaders of the Basque people (the last remaining indigenous group in Europe), she still is a leading authority on indigenous spirituality all over the world. She wrote a number of books, most notably *The Four-Fold Way*. I also recommend

The Tarot Handbook, which offers a profound interpretation of human evolution. A wonderful woman and a great teacher.

Reiki is perhaps the best known of all the different kinds of energy healing, but there are many others. *Hands of Light* by **Barbara Brennan** is a classic and a good place to start. **Anodea Judith** is the author of *Wheels of Life* and *Eastern Body, Western Mind*, which are both comprehensive guides to understanding the chakra system.

Richard Bartlett, D.C., N.D., is the author of several books and the inventor of **Matrix Energetics**, a powerful method of healing that works by collapsing the energetic field that is maintaining pain or illness. He teaches all over the world.

Finding good information about sex as a way of learning how to utilize and tap into energy flows is not easy, and much of the information is focused on intimacy within a relationship (which is important but different). The following organizations may be useful: **The Body Electric School, Skydancing Tantra,** and the **Human Awareness Institute.**

Up-to-date information on the **crop circles** can be found at **cropcircleconnector.com.** It's interesting to follow the reports on the new circles that are constantly being discovered all over the world, and the Internet is able to keep up with them much better than hard copy publications. There are also some books worth reading, such as *Crop Circles: The Greatest Mystery of Modern Times*, by **Lucy Pringle**, and *Mysterious Lights and Crop Circles*, by **Linda Moulton Howe**. Beware: British authorities seem to be very invested in belittling the crop circles, so there is some very biased and one-sided information circulating in the mainstream.

The ancient Celtic practice of **Wicca** is a kind of shamanism, and these days there are many modern day witches, or Wiccans, who practice alone or in covens. Many covens exist throughout the Western world, and although most of them are by invitation only, some are open. **Z Budapest** was the first of many Wiccan teachers to go public. **Starhawk** is a wonderful teacher who offers classes and has written several books, most notably *The Spiral Dance*.

Sandra Ingerman, M.A., is the author of several books on shamanism and related practices, and has produced five audio programs. She teaches all over the world. **The Power Path School of Shamanism**, founded by **Jose** and **Lena Stevens**, authors of *Secrets of Shamanism* and *The Power Path*, offers an extensive experiential curriculum based on years of study with indigenous shamans around the world. There are many other shamanic teachings and teachers: once again, go with what feels right to you.

Serge Kahili King is a Hawaiian who wrote *Urban Shaman* and other books. Hawaiian shamanism is more about love and cooperation than some other paths, and this book is particularly useful if you can't easily get out of a city setting.

Working with cards, or other methods of what is called **divination**, is something you can do by yourself, and you will often be amazed at the accuracy and profundity of the wisdom that comes through them. They can be great teachers. There are many different packs of **Tarot cards** available these days, as well as **angel cards, animal cards, oracle cards**, and **runes**.

Other books by Mikaya Heart

With the Sun in My Eyes: the true story of Maria Raindancer, a psychic reader and shamanic practitioner

iUniverse, 2007

(As of 2014, the first edition of this book is out of print; the second edition will be available shortly.)

With the Sun in My Eyes tells the inspiring true story of the shamanic healer and psychic, Maria Raindancer, providing an in-depth look into how she works with energy, exactly what she sees, and how she interprets her visions. In an intimate and conversational style, Ms. Heart weaves together many exciting stories she gathered from comprehensive interviews with Maria, her family, friends, and clients. The reader is left with a breathtaking awareness of the depth of Maria's ongoing relationship to spirit. Be prepared for an engaging read, as Maria battles demons and century-long familial curses; exorcises tenacious and often evil energies; removes dead entities which are still haunting the living; and acts as a go-between enabling dead people to talk with their still living families. She follows the constant instructions of spirit to the letter and never works without her intrepid power animals, Leopard and Raven.

Born with exceptional gifts, Maria trained from the age of fourteen with a Cheyenne teacher. She now does energy clearings, soul retrievals, psychic readings, extractions, and house blessings on a daily basis. The steps involved in her work are described in detail, from Maria's point of view as well as the client's. This is a holistic perspective on the life of a healer who works outside the physical arena, achieving remarkable results in realms unknown to most of us.

My Sweet Wild Dance

Dog Ear Publishing, 2009

This is the riveting story of Mikaya's personal journey from anger to joy. Using the name Chris, she describes growing up in the impoverished aristocracy of post-war Scotland. The black sheep of her family, she struggled against the confines of class and gender, searching for truth in an atmosphere where lies were the norm. As soon as she was old enough to escape her parents' stranglehold, she tried on many different personas, experimenting with drugs, free love, and anti-establishment politics. Always on the cutting edge of radical thought, she was active around environmental issues decades before they were common knowledge. Turning to Nature for solace, she moved to rural California, where she worked as a jill-of-all-trades, came out as a lesbian, and engaged in healing work centered around her sexuality. Facing her fears and finding love, she experienced many varied, riveting, and mind-expanding adventures that brought her to a place of deep compassion and forgiveness. Eventually, satisfied with nothing short of absolute freedom, she sold everything and took to the road, becoming the woman who follows the wind.

Mikaya Heart knows how to dance her own sweet, wild dance, and she offers a compelling picture of the rewards of living one's personal truth. The path she has forged through the jungle of life is an inspiration to anyone who is looking for the true meaning of love in our changing world.

The Ultimate Guide to Orgasm for Women: How to Become Orgasmic for a Lifetime

Cleis Press, 2011

(This book was originally published in 1998 as *When the Earth Moves: Women and Orgasm*).

The result of dozens of comprehensive interviews as well as many in-depth questionnaires, this book is a thorough, realistic and nonjudgmental examination of what we generally call orgasm. Owning our desires should be neither embarrassing nor uncomfortable. Nor should they be subject to anyone else's moral judgment of what is right or wrong, good or bad, normal or abnormal. Combining communication and information is the key. By shrugging off the taboos against talking about our preferences and experiences when we're being sexual, we will take the first and most important steps toward ensuring our own fulfillment. *The Ultimate Guide to Orgasm for Women* is an unflinchingly honest, responsible, and thoroughly comprehensive exploration of female sexuality. Topics include physical types of orgasm, such as electrical, flying, pounding, deep, waves, and blips; orgasm as an emotional release; the "elusive orgasm" and why some women have difficulty having one; how often we fake them and why; masturbation; multiple orgasms; the male-female dichotomy; penetration and the G-spot; defining the erotic; and the joy of sex toys.